Harpsichord & fortepiano

Harpsichord & fortepiano
Harpsichord & fortepiano was founded in 1973 by Edgar Hunt as The *English Harpsichord Magazine*, adopting the current title in 1987. It is published twice a year, in the Spring and Autumn, and is available worldwide

Editor
Francis Knights, Fitzwilliam College, Cambridge, email fk240@cam.ac.uk

Publisher, Advertising and Subscriptions
Peacock Press Ltd, Scout Bottom Farm, Mytholmroyd, Hebden Bridge, Yorkshire HX7 5JX, United Kingdom, tel 01422 882751

Website
www.hfmagazine.info
See the website to view the archive, style guide, ad rates and to renew subscriptions

Design and Artwork
DM Design and Print

ISBN: 978-1-914934-71-1
ISSN: 1463-0036

COMPLETE INDEX, 1973-2023

Compiled by Francis Knights

3	Issue Index, 1973-2023
31	Subject Index
31	Instruments
35	Keyboards and Makers
38	Stringing, Tuning and Maintenance
41	Repertoire
46	Performance and Teaching
49	Collections and Organizations
50	Interviews and Profiles
53	Obituaries
54	Miscellaneous
56	Author Index

Cover image:
Spinet by Edward Blunt (1704), by kind permission of David Hackett

ISSUE INDEX, 1973-2023

This chronological Index covers every issue of the *English Harpsichord Magazine* and *Harpsichord & fortepiano*, vols. i-xxviii, and includes all of the content apart from reports, reviews and advertisements. For a Subject Index (including Interviews and Obituaries) and for an Author Index of articles, see below. The history of the magazine can be found at Francis Knights, '50 years of *Harpsichord & Fortepiano*', xxviii/1 (Autumn 2023), pp.4-7.

The Harpsichord Magazine, i/1 (October 1973)

'Editorial', Edgar Hunt, p.1
'George Malcolm, C.B.E.: An Interview', Edgar Hunt, pp.2-5
'A Visit to Robert Goble', [Edgar Hunt], p.6
'Early English Harpsichord Building: A Reassessment', Thomas McGeary, pp.7-19, 30
'The Broadwood Books: I', Charles Mould, pp.19-23
'Harpsichord Building: I. Preparing the Action for Voicing', Dave Law, pp.23-25
'The Harpsichordist's Bookshelf [Reviews]', Maria Boxall, pp.27-29
'The Harpsichord Scene', pp.29-30

The English Harpsichord Magazine, i/2 (April 1974)

'Editorial', Edgar Hunt, p.33
'Gustav Leonhardt: An Interview', Edgar Hunt, pp.34-35, 63
'An Early-Eighteenth-century Harpsichord by Thomas Barton', Charles Mould, pp.36-38
'The Fretted Clavichord', Michael Thomas, pp.39-47
'The Broadwood Books; II', Charles Mould, pp.47-53
'Harpsichord Building: II. Voicing and Regulating', Dave Law, pp.53-57
'Correspondence', Michael Thomas, pp.57-59
'The Harpsichordist's Bookshelf [Reviews]', Edgar Hunt, Maria Boxall, pp.59-61
'The Harpsichord Scene', pp.61-63

The English Harpsichord Magazine, i/3 (October 1974)

'Editorial', Edgar Hunt, p.65
'Kenneth Gilbert: An Interview', Edgar Hunt, pp.66-69
'The English Virginals: I', Richard Luckett, pp.69-72
'Early French Harpsichords', Michael Thomas, pp.73-84
'Quick Jacks for Amateurs', P. Deen, pp.84-86
'The Harpsichordist's Bookshelf [Reviews]', Edgar Hunt, pp.86-89
'The Harpsichord Scene', pp.89-91
'Harpsichords on Record [Reviews]', Maria Boxall, p.91

'Obituaries: Dr. Thornton Lofthouse; Philip James, C.B.E.', Ruth Dyson, Edgar Hunt, pp.91-92
'Correspondence', Edwin M. Ripin, Michael Thomas, Peter Thornton, Tom McGeary, pp.93-94

The English Harpsichord Magazine, i/4 (April 1975)

'Editorial', Edgar Hunt, p.97
'Frank Hubbard Interviewed', Tom McGeary, pp.98-105
'The "Incy Wincy Spider"', Maria Boxall, pp.106-108 [see also i/5, pp.154-155]
'Venetian Harpsichords', Michael Thomas, pp.109-120
'The Harpsichord Scene', pp.121-123
'The Harpsichordist's Bookshelf [Reviews]', Edgar Hunt, p.125
'Correspondence', John Barnes, Herbert A. Kellner, Michael Thomas, Jean Maurer, Maria Boxall, pp.126-127

The English Harpsichord Magazine, i/5 (October 1975)

'Editorial', Edgar Hunt, p.129
'Ruth Dyson, an Interview', [Edgar Hunt], pp.130-132
'Elementary Harpsichord Technique', Roy Truby, pp.132-134
'The Archicembalo of Nicola Vincentino', Marco Tiella, pp.134-144
'The Development of the Tuning and Tone Colour of an Instrument made in Venice about 1500', Michael Thomas, pp.145-155
'[Two Preludes]', [Maria Boxall, continued from i/4, pp.106-108]
'Obituaries: John Challis; Thomas Goff', p.155
'The Harpsichord Scene', pp.156-159
'Correspondence', Edwin M. Ripin, James H. Meyer, Michael Thomas, Timothy Llewellyn, David Jewell, pp.159-161
'The Harpsichordist's Bookshelf [Reviews]', Maria Boxall, Edgar Hunt, pp.161-162
'Harpsichords on Record [Reviews]', Maria Boxall, pp.162-163

The English Harpsichord Magazine, i/6 (April 1976)

'Editorial', Edgar Hunt, p.165
'Igor Kipnis: A Meeting', [Edgar Hunt], pp.166-167
'Girolamo Diruta's "Il Transilvano" and the Early Italian Keyboard Tradition', Maria Boxall, pp.168-172
'The Wearing Properties of Harpsichord Plectra', M. R. Levoi and R. P. Williams, pp.172-174
'The Tunings and Pitch of Early Clavichords', Michael Thomas, pp.175-180
'The Harpsichord Scene', pp.180-185

'Obituaries: Edwin M. Ripin, Frank Hubbard', John Barnes, p.185
'Correspondence', John Barnes, D. M. Hoogland, pp.187-188
'Music for Harpsichord [Reviews]', Maria Boxall, pp.188-189
'A Practical Guide to Thorough Bass (1808), Chapter 9', A. F. C. Kollman, p.190

The English Harpsichord Magazine, i/7 (October 1976)

'Editorial', Edgar Hunt, p.193
'The Harpsichord at the Courtauld Institute', Michael Thomas, pp.194-197
'The Instrumental Museum – Lisbon', L. A. Esteves Pereria, pp.197-198
'An Interesting Early Forte-Piano', C. F. Colt, pp.198-201
'Tuning and Temperament', Edgar Hunt, pp.201-204
'The Harpsichordist's Bookshelf [Reviews]', Maria Boxall, pp.204-205
'Music for Harpsichord [Reviews]', Maria Boxall, pp.205-207
'Harpsichords on Record [Reviews]', Maria Boxall, p.207
'Correspondence', Mark Lindley, Herbert A. Kellner, p.207
'The Harpsichord Scene', pp.208-210
'Notes and Corrections to former Articles and New Information', Michael Thomas,
    pp.211-219

The English Harpsichord Magazine, i/8 (April 1977)

'Editorial', Edgar Hunt, p.221
'Ton Koopman: A Meeting', [Edgar Hunt], p.222
'The Performer's Approach to Scarlatti', Richard Lester, pp.223-226
'The Claviorganum in England', Stephen Wessel, pp.226-233
'Further Thoughts and Notes', Michael Thomas, pp.223-235
'Tuning and Temperaments', Roy Truby, p.235
'The Harpsichord Scene', Maria Boxall, S. L., pp.236-238
'Correspondence', John Henry van der Meer, Herbert A. Kellner, J. A. Richard,
    pp.238-239
'Harpsichords on Record [Reviews], Maria Boxall, p.239-240
'A Harpsichord Method [review]', Michael Thomas, pp.240-243
'The Harpsichordist's Bookshelf [Reviews]', Maria Boxall, pp.243-245
'Keyboard Music [review]', Maria Boxall, p.245
'Inscriptions on Harpsichords', Edgar Hunt, pp.245-237

The English Harpsichord Magazine, ii/1 (October 1977)

'Editorial', Edgar Hunt, p.1
'Maria Boxall Interviewed', David Lasocki, pp.2-4
'"My Lady Nevell's Book" and Old Fingerings', Ton Koopman, pp.5-10
'Thoughts on Scarlatti's Essercizi per Gravicembalo', Richard Lester, pp.10-12, 17-18

'Tuning Systems for 12-note Keyboard Instruments', Mark Lindley, pp.13-15
'The Harpsichord Scene', pp.18-20, 28
'A Duet by Nicholas Carlton completed Dr. Bernard Rose', pp.20-21
'The Harpsichordist's Bookshelf [Reviews]', pp.21-22
'Harpsichord Tone Colour', John Paul, *The English Harpsichord Magazine*, ii/1 (October 1977), pp.22-26
'For Two to Play', Maria Boxall, *The English Harpsichord Magazine*, ii/1 (October 1977), pp.26-27

The English Harpsichord Magazine, ii/2 (April 1978)

'Editorial', Edgar Hunt, p.29
'An Octave Harpsichord at the Instrumental Museum - Lisbon', L. A. Esteves Pereira, pp.30-32
'Was Bach a Mathematician?', Herbert Anton Kellner, pp.32-36
'Organ Restoration in Florence', Rudolph Kremer, pp.37-39
'A Harpsichord from Switzerland', Will Bruggmann, pp.40-44
'Correspondence', R. Kitchener, p.44
'The Harpsichord Scene', pp.45-51
'The Harpsichordist's Bookshelf [Reviews]', Edgar Hunt, p.53
'Music for Harpsichord [review]', Maria Boxall, p.53
'Harpsichords on Record [Reviews]', Maria Boxall, pp.53-54
'Volume 1 – October 1973-April 1977: Index', pp.55-56

The English Harpsichord Magazine, ii/3 (October 1978)

'Editorial', Edgar Hunt, p.57
'Harpsichord Construction in Canada', Barry Ainslie, pp.58-62
'Thoughts on the Restoration of Harpsichords', Michael Thomas, pp.62-67
'Bach and the German Clavier', D. E. Dodge, pp.67-71
'New Light on the Early Italian Keyboard Tradition' Maria Boxall, pp.71-72
'Paul Hofhaimer', pp.72-73
'The Harpsichordist's Bookshelf [Reviews]', Edgar Hunt, pp.73-74
'Correspondence', J. H. van der Meer, Peter W. Redstone, Christopher Kite, Maria Boxall, p.74
'Harpsichords on Record [Reviews]', Maria Boxall, pp.74-75
'The Harpsichord Scene', pp.76-79
'Early Keyboards in the Galpin Society Journal: A Check List of Articles – Part 1', p.80

The English Harpsichord Magazine, ii/4 (April 1979)

'Editorial', Edgar Hunt, p.81
'Luis Gonzalez Uriol Interviewed', Susanne Shapiro, pp.82-83

'The Upright Harpsichord', Michael Thomas, pp.84-92
'The Nineteenth-Century View of the Old Harpsichord', P. Sween, pp.92-95
'The Harpsichord Scene', pp.96-98
'The Harpsichordist's Bookshelf [Reviews]', Maria Boxall, Edgar Hunt, pp.99-100
'Music for Harpsichord [review]', Maria Boxall, pp.100-101
'Harpsichords on Record [Reviews]', Maria Boxall, pp.101-102
'Correspondence', David J. Way, Colin Booth, L. A. Esteves Pereira, pp.102-104
'As we go to Press', Edgar Hunt, p.105
'Early Keyboards in the Galpin Society Journal: A Check List of Articles – Part 2', p.107

The English Harpsichord Magazine, ii/5 (October 1979)

'Editorial', Edgar Hunt, p.109
'The Pleyel Harpsichord', J. A. Richard, pp.110-113
'Master Brian his Virginall [Lodewijk Theeuwes]', Brian Morgan, pp.114-115
'The Identity of Bach's Clavier', D. E. Dodge, pp.116-119
'The Harpsichord Scene', pp.119-123 [see also *The English Harpsichord Magazine*, ii/6 (April 1980), pp.141-143]
'Correspondence', D. E. Dodge, Herbert Anton Kellner, p.123
'A Modern Upright Harpsichord', John Paul, pp.124-125
'The Harpsichordist's Bookshelf [Reviews]', Maria Boxall, J. G. [Jonathan Garland], p.127
'Harpsichords on Record [Reviews]', Maria Boxall, pp.127-129
'and Organs [Reviews]', J. G. [Jonathan Garland], p.129
'Corrette on Stringing and Tuning', Edgar Hunt, pp.130-132

The English Harpsichord Magazine, ii/6 (April 1980)

'Editorial', Edgar Hunt, p.133
'The John Loosemore Centre for Organ and Early Music', Jonathan Garland, pp.134-136
'Das Wohltemperierte Clavier: Tuning & Musical Structure', Herbert Anton Kellner, pp.137-140
'L'Orgue et le Clavecin', pp.141-143
'The Harpsichord Scene', Maria Boxall, Marco Tiella, pp.144-151
'The Fourth London Exhibition of Early Musical Instruments', p.151
'The Harpsichordist's Bookshelf [Reviews]', Edgar Hunt, pp.151-153
'Harpsichords on Record [Reviews]', Maria Boxall, S. Shapiro, pp.153-154
'and Organs [Reviews]', Jonathan Garland, pp.154-155
'Harpsichord Music Reviewed', S. Shapiro, Jonathan Garland, pp.155-156

The English Harpsichord Magazine, **ii/7 (October 1980)**

'Editorial', Edgar Hunt, p.157
'Harpsichords which have been found recently in France', Michael Thomas, pp.158-163
'Peter Redstone: Harpsichord Maker', [Edgar Hunt], pp.163-164
'The Harpsichord Scene', Jonathan Garland, Edgar Hunt, Maria Boxall, pp.165-169
'The Harpsichordist's Bookshelf [Reviews]', Maria Boxall, S. J. L., pp.169-171
'Harpsichord Music Reviewed', Maria Boxall, p.171
'Harpsichords on Record [Reviews]', Maria Boxall, Edgar Hunt, pp.171-174
'and Organs [Reviews]', Jonathan Garland, pp.174-175

The English Harpsichord Magazine, **ii/8 (April 1981)**

'Editorial', Edgar Hunt, p.177
'The Harpsichord Master of 1697 and its relationship to contemporary instruction & playing', Maria Boxall, pp.178-183
'The Mathematical Architecture of Bach's Goldberg Variations', Herbert Anton Kellner, pp.183-189
'The Harpsichord Master of 1697', Maria Boxall, pp.178-183
'A Harpsichord Odyssey (1)', Edgar Hunt, pp.190-194
'Harpsichords on Record [Reviews]', Maria Boxall, p.195
'and Organs [Reviews]', Jonathan Garland, pp.195-196
'Book Reviews: pp.196-197
'Harpsichord Music Reviewed', Maria Boxall, Jonathan Garland, p.199
'The Harpsichord Scene', Jonathan Garland, Edgar Hunt, Maria Boxall, p.200
'Obituary: Hans Neupert', p.200

The English Harpsichord Magazine, **iii/1 (October 1981)**

'Volume 1 [recte 2] – October 1977-April 1981: Index', pp.i-ii
'Editorial', Edgar Hunt, p.1
'The Haward Harpsichord at Knole', Dennis Woolley, pp.2-3
'A Harpsichord Odyssey (II)', Edgar Hunt, pp.4-7
'The Harpsichord Scene', Herbert Anton Kellner, pp.8-10
'The Harpsichordist's Bookshelf [Reviews]', Edgar Hunt, p.11
'Harpsichords on Record [Reviews]', Jonathan Garland, pp.12-14
'Correspondence', Thomas McGeary, G. J. Causon, pp.14-16
'Telemann's Harpsichord Music', Edgar Hunt, p.16

The English Harpsichord Magazine, iii/2 (April 1982)

'Editorial', Edgar Hunt, p.17
'Early Eighteenth-Century English Harpsichord Tuning and Stringing', Thomas McGeary, pp.18-22
'The Harpsichord Scene', Maria Boxall, pp.23-25
'Malcolm Proud', p.25
'The Harpsichordist's Library [Reviews]', Maria Boxall, pp.26-30
'More Harpsichord Music Reviewed', Jonathan Garland, pp.30-31
'Correspondence', R. G. Murray, p.31
'Obituary: Elizabeth Goble', p.32

The English Harpsichord Magazine, iii/3 (October 1982)

'Editorial', Edgar Hunt, p.33
'Editor's Note', Edgar Hunt, p.34
'The Musical Mechanisms of Arnaut de Zwolle', John Lester, pp.35-41
'David Law: Harpsichord Maker', pp.41-43
'Harpsichords at Christie's', p.43
'Recent Harpsichord Restorations (I)', Michael Thomas, pp.45-48
'The Harpsichordist's Bookshelf [Reviews]', p.49
'Harpsichord Music Reviewed', F. O. M., pp.49-51
'Harpsichords on Record [Reviews]', p.51
'The Harpsichord Scene', Rodger Mirrey, pp.52-56

The English Harpsichord Magazine, iii/4 (April 1983)

'Editorial', Edgar Hunt, p.57
'Ammerbach's 1583 Exercises', Mark Lindley, pp.58-66
'A Forte-piano at the Instrumental Museum – Lisbon', L. A. Esteves Pereria, pp.67-70
'Recent Harpsichord Restorations (II)', Michael Thomas, pp.71-72, 79
'Two small Organs revived', L. A. Esteves Pereria, pp.73-76
'The Harpsichordist's Bookshelf [Reviews]', pp.77-79
'The Virginal at the Museum of London', Edgar Hunt, p.79
'Obituary: Mary Potts', p.79
Record Reviews: p.80

The English Harpsichord Magazine, iii/5 (October 1983)

'Editorial', Edgar Hunt, p.81
'The Position of Grace Signs in MS. Sources of English Virginal Music', Desmond Hunter, pp.82-91
Reviews: p.91

'Boston Early Music Festival & Exhibition', pp.92-94
'Bruges 1983 Harpsichord & Fortepiano Week', Michael Heale, pp.94-96
'On choosing a Harpsichord', Edgar Hunt, pp.97-98
'Harpsichord Building: Preparing the Action for Voicing', Dave Law, pp.98-102, 96
'The Harpsichord Scene', pp.103, 96

The English Harpsichord Magazine, iii/6 (April 1984)

'Editorial', Edgar Hunt, p.105
'An Early Clavycytherium Reconstructed', Peter Bavington, pp.106-111
'A Visit to John Rawson', pp.112-115
'Harpsichords...with all the different-siz'd wire used in that instrument (I)', J. J. K. Rhodes and W. R. Thomas, pp.116-118
'Another Burkat Tchudi Harpichord Found', L. A. Esteves Pereria, p.119
'The Harpsichord Scene', pp.120-121, 127
'Harpsichords on Record [Reviews]', p.122
'The Harpsichordist's Library [Reviews]', Herbert Anton Kellner, pp.122-127
'Early Keyboards in the Galpin Society Journal: A Check List of Articles – Part 3', p.128

The (English) Harpsichord Magazine, iii/7 (October 1984)

'Editorial', Edgar Hunt, p.105
'Harpsichords...with all the different-siz'd wire used in that instrument (II)', J. J. K. Rhodes and W. R. Thomas, pp.130-133
'Is there an Enigma in Werckmeister's "Musicalische Temperatur"?', Herbert Anton Kellner, pp.134-136
'The Harpsichord Scene', pp.137-140
'Harpsichords on Record [Reviews]', pp.141-142
'and Organs [Reviews]', p.142
'Musings on the Muselar', Edgar Hunt, pp.143-144
'The Harpsichordist's Bookshelf [Reviews]', p.144

The (English) Harpsichord Magazine, iii/8 (April 1985)

'Editorial', Edgar Hunt, p.145
'One typographical Enigma in Werckmeister, "Musicalische Temperatur"', Herbert Anton Kellner, pp.146-151
'Harpsichords...with all the different-siz'd wire used in that instrument (III)', J. J. K. Rhodes and W. R. Thomas, pp.152-154
'Organs of Upper Austria', p.154
'Early Keyboard Fingerings: A select Bibliography', Mark Lindley, pp.155-161 [see also *EHM* iv/1 (October 1985), p.15]

'The Harpsichord Scene', Roy Truby, pp.162-165
Record Review: p.165
'The Harpsichordist's Library [Reviews]', Maria Boxall, Edgar Hunt, pp.122-127

The (English) Harpsichord Magazine, iv/1 (October 1985)

'Editorial', Edgar Hunt, p.1
'Further Light on Early Keyboard Fingerings', Desmond Hunter, pp.2-7
'Did Werckmeister already know the tuning of J. S. Bach for the "48"?', Herbert Anton Kellner, pp.7-11 [see also Erratum in *EHM*, iv/2 (1986), p.32]
'The Harpsichordist's Bookshelf [Reviews]', pp.11-13
'The Harpsichord Scene', Herbert Anton Kellner, pp.13-15
'Harpsichords on Record', p.16
'Volume 3 – October 1981-April 1985: Index', pp.[17-18]

The English Harpsichord Magazine, iv/2 (1986)

'Editorial', Edgar Hunt, p.17
'The temperament for Bach's "48"', Michael Thomas, pp.18-21
'How Bach quantified his well-tempered tuning within the FOUR DUETS', Herbert Anton Kellner, pp.21-27
'Keyboards on Record', pp.28-29
'Harpsichord Music', pp.29-30
'The Harpsichordist's Bookshelf [Reviews]', p.30
'The Harpsichord Scene', Herbert Anton Kellner, pp.31-32
'Obituary: J. J. K. Rhodes', P. Holden, p.32
'Erratum', Herbert Anton Kellner, p.32
'The Fretted Clavichord', Michael Thomas, pp.33-44
Book Review: p.[45]

The Harpsichord and Fortepiano Magazine, iv/3 (April 1987)

'Editorial', Warwick Henry Cole, p.45
'A Seventeenth Century French Harpsichord', Chris Nobbs, pp.46-51 [see also *HF* iv/4 (October 1987), pp.102-103]
'Playing Mozart On The Fortepiano', Christopher Kite, pp.52-55
'Towards Boalch III', Charles Mould, pp.56-59
'International Harpsichord and Fortepiano Week', Kenneth Mobbs, pp.60-62
'Collections – Finchcocks', Warwick Henry Cole, pp.63-65
'News, Reviews and Previews': Malcolm Rose, Simon Heighes, Kenneth Mobbs, Peter McMullin, Warwick Henry Cole, pp.66-72
Music Supplement: Domenico Alberti, Sonata (1749) [see also *HF* iv/4 (October 1987), pp.103-104]

The Harpsichord and Fortepiano Magazine, **iv/4 (October 1987)**

'Editorial', Warwick Henry Cole, p.73
'An Interview With Melvyn Tan', Warwick Henry Cole, pp.74-78
'Americus Backers: Original Forte Piano Maker', Warwick Henry Cole, pp.79-85
'St. Cecilia's Hall And The Russell Collection', John Raymond, pp.86-91
'The London Sale Rooms', Michael Cole, pp.91-93
'The Boston Early Music Festival 1987', Warwick Henry Cole, pp.94-97
'News, Reviews and Previews': Maria Boxall, Warwick Henry Cole, Bernard Harrison, Ewan West, Simon Heighes, pp.97-102
'A Seventeenth Century French Harpsichord?', Chris Nobbs, pp.102-103
'H & FM Music Supplement [Domenico Alberti]', pp.103-104

The Harpsichord and Fortepiano Magazine, **iv/5 (April 1988)**

'Editorial', Warwick Henry Cole, p.105
'Aspects of Thorough Bass', David Roblou, pp.106-112
'Viscount Fitzwilliam and the English "Scarlatti Sect"', Gerald Gifford, pp.113-116
'The Pedal Harpsichord – A Recent Reconstruction', Colin Booth, pp.117-120
'The London Salerooms', Michael Cole, pp.121-124
'Eighth London Exhibition of Early Musical Instruments 1987', Kenneth Mobbs, pp.125-126
'News, Reviews and Previews': Michael Cole, Warwick Henry Cole, Peter McMullin, Kenneth Mobbs, Martin Souter, p.127

The Harpsichord and Fortepiano Magazine, **iv/6 (October 1988)**

'Editorial', Warwick Henry Cole, p.133
'On the New Fortepiano in Contemporary German Musical Writings', Katalin Komlos, pp.134-139
'Two Harpsichords by Elpidio Gregori', William Dow, pp.140-145
'An Interview with Maggie Cole', pp.146-149
'From Pepin to Walter [NEMA Conference 1988]', Peter Bavington, pp.150-155
'News, Reviews and Previews': Michael Cole, Warwick Henry Cole, Martin Souter, pp.156-163
'Correspondence', Mike Cooper, pp.163-164
'H & FM Music Supplement [George Frederic Pinto]', pp.164-165

The Harpsichord and Fortepiano Magazine, **iv/7 (April 1989)**

'Editorial', Warwick Henry Cole, p.167
'Trevor Pinnock Interviewed', pp.168-172
'The Keyboard Music of Hugh Facy', Desmond Hunter, pp.173-177

'The Metropolitan Museum of Art', Laurence Libin, pp.178-184
'News, Reviews and Previews': Michael Cole, Warwick Henry Cole, Giles Edwards, pp.156-163

Harpsichord and fortepiano, v/1 (October 1994)

'A Note from the Editor', David Bray, p.2
'Soundboard: News in the early keyboard world', pp.3-6
'Obituaries: David Jacques Way, Peter Whale, Christopher Kite', p.7
'The Challenge of New Music', Jane Chapman, pp.7-13
'Letters to the Editor', John Harley, p.14
'The Hudiksvall Mietke', Andreas Kilström, pp.15-18
'Interpretation with respect: An interview with Christophe Rousset', David Bray, pp.19-21
'Monteverdi on the road', Simon Neal, pp.22-25
'Conservation conversation', Mimi Waitzman, p.26
'A Bone of Contention: Should we stop restoring and playing original instruments?', Göran Grahn, pp.27-28
'…Or should good restoration still be carried out?', David Winston, p.29
'A Collection in distress? The Colt Clavier Collection at 50', pp.30-32
'Book Reviews: Paul Irvin, Igor Kipnis, Kah-Ming Ng, Sophie Yates, pp.33-35
Disc Reviews: Stephen Patrick, John Henry, Howard A. Fenton, David Bray, Sebastien Dédis, pp.36-40
'Care of…: Regular maintenance of your keyboard', Mimi Waitzman, pp.41-42
'Tail Ends: Pitching it right', Jackson Amers, p.43

Harpsichord and fortepiano, v/2 (April 1995)

'A Note from the Editor', David Bray, p.2
'Soundboard: News in the early keyboard world', pp.3-6
'Stars, the Chorus and a Pantomine Horse [auction report]', Peter Bavington, pp.7-10
'Back to Bach: *Das Wohltemperirte Clavier* revisited', Stephen Daw, pp.11-15
'Letters to the Editor', Edgar Hunt, Carl Sloane, Ray Hands, p.16
'"Catching the rhythm": An interview with Andreas Staier', David Bray, pp.17-19
'"Take Six Eggs…": Making and using egg tempera on harpsichord soundboards', Jenny Haylett, pp.20-22
'Do we know how to read Urtext editions? *or* the case of the Missing Dot', Malcolm Bilson, pp.23-30
'Friends of the Fortepiano: The Accademia Bartolomeo Cristofori', Stefano Fiuzzi, pp.31-32
'Ligurian harpsichord investigated', Maurizio Tarrini, pp.33-34
Book Review: Andrew McCrea, p.35

Disc Reviews: Lee Ridgway, Sebastien Dédis, Amy Foster, Howard A. Fenton,
    Stephen Patrick, John Henry, Howard A. Fenton, Declan Deuchar, pp.36-39
'Care of…: Regular maintenance of your keyboard', Mimi Waitzman, pp.40-41
'Tail Ends: The text and nothing but the text', Jackson Amers, p.44

Harpsichord and fortepiano, v/3 (October 1995)

'A Note from the Editor', David Bray, p.2
'Soundboard: News in the early keyboard world', pp.3-5
'Japanese Performer Abroad [Motoko Nabeshima]', p.6
'A Question of Cultural Identity', Motoko Nabeshima', pp.7-10
'PitchMan: Budget-priced electronic tuner for historical temperaments', Dave Gayman,
    pp.11-14
'The Cent System: with an easy method of calculation', Carl Sloane, pp.15-16
'Mean as they come: Clues in the elucidation of Handel's harpsichord temperament',
    Carl Sloane, pp.17-19 [see also *Harpsichord and fortepiano*, vi/2 (November 1997),
    p.35]
'"A music of surprise and delight": An interview with James Nicolson', Dave Gayman,
    pp.20-23
'*Philibuster*: New music for the fortepiano', Marc Reichow and Richard Sims, pp.23-29
'Letters to the Editor', Herbert Anton Kellner, Stephen Daw, Peter Katin, p.30
'Soundboard painting: The Traditional Touch', Mary Mobbs, pp.31-32
Book Review:Amy Foster, p.33
Disc Reviews: John Henry, Sebastien Dédis, Pamela Nash, Declan Deuchar, Amy Foster,
James Morris, pp.34-36
'Care of…: Regular maintenance of your keyboard', Mimi Waitzman, pp.38-39
'Tail Ends: You are what you wear', Jackson Amers, p.40

Harpsichord and fortepiano, vi/1 (May 1997)

'A Note from the Editors', Alison and Peter Holloway, p.2
'Soundboard: News in the early keyboard world', pp.3-6
'Dance to the Music of Time [Delius, *Dance for Harpsichord*]', Penelope Cave, pp.7-9
'Egarr, to please [interview with Richard Egarr]', Alison Holloway, pp.10-12
'Fortepiano kapsels old and new', Martha Goodway, pp.13-16
'An American in Paris [interview with Kenneth Weiss]', Alison Holloway, pp.17-19
'Did Couperin ever play a trill before the beat?', Claudio Di Veroli, pp.20-22
'Handel's eight great suites for harpsichord', Gwilym Beechey, pp.24-26
'The vital rôle of humidity', Martin Robertson, p.27
Book Review: peter Holloway, pp.28-30
Disc Reviews: Richard Leigh Harris, Peter Holloway, pp.31-34
Music Reviews: Peter Holloway, pp.35-36

Harpsichord and fortepiano, vi/2 (November 1997)

'A Note from the Editors', Alison and Peter Holloway, p.2
'Soundboard: News in the early keyboard world', pp.3-5
'A Performance Practice for the 21st Century: interview with Jane Chapman, Part One',
    Pamela Nash, pp.6-10 [and see *HF*, vii/1 (June 1998), pp.23-28]
'Isolde Ahlgrimm and Vienna's Historic Keyboard Revival', Peter Watchorn, pp.10-17
    [and see 'Isolde Ahlgrimm: discography, performers, publications and
    instruments', Peter Watchorn, *HF*, vii/1 (June 1998), pp.14-22]
'An interview with Sharona Joshua', Alison Holloway, pp.18-19
'Early keyboards in Argentina', Claudio Di Veroli, pp.20-21
'The Brandenburg Concertos: A New Interpretation', Philip Pickett, pp.22-32
'An interview with Olga Tverskaya', Alison Holloway, pp.33-34
'Handel's Temperament – A Revised View', Carl Sloane, p.35
'Obituary: Ruth Dyson', Penelope Cave, p.36
'Festival Reviews: Carey Beebe, Réjean Poirier, pp.37-39
Concert Reviews: Martin Perkins, Peter Holloway, pp.39-40
Music Reviews: Richard Leigh Harris, Peter Holloway, pp.41-43
Disc Reviews: Penelope Cave, Peter Holloway, Martin Perkins, Gwilym Beechey,
    pp.44-48

Harpsichord and fortepiano, vii/1 (June 1998)

'A Note from the Editors', Alison and Peter Holloway, p.2
'Soundboard: News in the early keyboard world', pp.3-4
'Keyboard Instruments in Haydn's Vienna', Richard Maunder, pp.5-10
'An interview with Ronald Brautigam', Alison Holloway, pp.11-13
'Isolde Ahlgrimm: discography, performers, publications and instruments', Peter
    Watchorn, pp.14-22
'A Performance Practice for the 21st Century: interview with Jane Chapman, Part Two',
    Pamela Nash, pp.23-28
'Christoph Benjamin Schmidtchen and his Small Keyboard Tutor', Gwilym Beechey,
    pp.29-34
'Underground Movement [Harley Foundation]', Alison Holloway, pp.35-38
Book Review: Penelope Cave, p.39
Music Reviews: Richard Leigh Harris, Gwilym Beechey, Penelope Cave, pp.40-43
Disc Reviews: Peter Holloway, Richard Leigh Harris, pp.44-48

Harpsichord and fortepiano, vii/1 (Winter 1998)

'A Note from the Editors', Alison and Peter Holloway, p.2
'Soundboard: News in the early keyboard world', pp.3-4
'The Naked Truth: Composing for the Harpsichord', Kevin Malone, pp.5-9

'Behind the Mask: Continuo in Monteverdi's *L'Orfeo*', Philip Pickett, pp.10-16
'"…dovendosi sonare piu piano, che sij possibile…": style in Italian harpsichord basso continuo realization', Giulia Nuti, pp.18-26
'Techniques of Baroque Accompaniment', Robert Webb, pp.28-34
'*pian'e fortino*: The Neumeyer Collection and its curator', Alison Holloway, pp.35-38
'Bach Transcribed: A Study in Two Parts', Pamela Nash, pp.39-43
Book Review:Gwilym Beechey, p.44
'Music Review', Peter Holloway, pp.44-34
Concert Reviews: Peter Holloway, Alison Holloway, pp.45-48
Disc Reviews: Penelope Cave, Richard Leigh Harris, Peter Holloway, Martin Perkins, Pamela Nash, Gwilym Beechey, Peter Watchorn, Kevin Malone, pp.48-60
'[Obituary:] Geraint Jones 1917-1998', Gwilym Beechey, p.60

Harpsichord and fortepiano, viii/1 (Autumn 1999)

'A Note from the Editors', Alison and Peter Holloway, p.2
'Dussek, Broadwood and the Additional Keys', Mora Carroll, pp.3-10
'Igor Kipnis talks to Elaine Hoffman Baruch', pp.11-22
'Bach Transcribed: Part Two', Pamela Nash, pp.23-26
Book Review:Richard Maunder, p.27
Disc Reviews: Richard Leigh Harris, Pamela Nash, Gwilym Beechey, Tristram Pugin, Penelope Cave, Peter Holloway, pp.27-35
'Festival Reviews: Peter Watchorn, pp.35-39

Harpsichord and fortepiano, viii/2 (Spring 2000)

'A Note from the Editors', Alison and Peter Holloway, pp.2-3
'Soundboard: News in the early keyboard world', pp.4-5
'Pick up your fingers, prick up your ears', Gary Blaise, pp.6-18
'Bach Transcribed: Part Three', Pamela Nash, pp.19-23
'John Field (1782-1837) and his Piano Music', Gwilym Beechey, pp.24-27
'Inégalité and Rameau's Concerts: a case of "Ille dixit"?', Claudio Di Veroli, pp.28-34
Music Reviews: Gwilym Beechey, Richard Maunder, Peter Holloway, pp.35-36
Concert Reviews: Peter Holloway, Alison Holloway, pp.36-38
Disc Reviews: Pamela Nash, Richard Maunder, Gwilym Beechey, Peter Holloway, pp.38-43

Harpsichord and fortepiano, ix/1 (Spring 2001)

'A Note from the Editors', Alison and Peter Holloway, p.2
'Renaissance Harpsichord Renaissance: Philip Pickett's approach to performance practice and why he commissioned the Trasuntino copy', Alison Holloway, pp.3-6

'The 1531 Trasuntino Harpsichord in a Universal European Pitch System', Nicholas Mitchell, pp.7-13
'Losing their heads?', Andrew Stewart, pp.14-15
'Windebank's Virginall: A Lost Ruckers Harpsichord', Paula Woods, pp.16-23
'The Authority of the Bevin table in the interpretation of ornament signs in Elizabethan virginal music', Asako Hirabayashi, pp.24-30
Disc Reviews: Penelope Cave, p.31
'Classical Studies – 1', Peter Holloway, pp.32-40

Harpsichord and fortepiano, ix/2 (Summer 2001)

'A Note from the Editors', Alison and Peter Holloway, p.2
'The Broadwood Trust: Grand Finale', Katrina Burnett, pp.3-7
'Jan Ladislav Dussek and his music for the extended keyboard compass', Mora Carroll, pp.8-15
'Practice Matters: Preparing the performing score to ease communication between the notes, the brain and the fingers', Penelope Cave, pp.16-19
'Some rare sources of Georgian harpsichord music in the Library of Arnold Dolmetsch (1858-1940)', Gerald Gifford, pp.20-25
'Book Reviews: Michael Cole, Peter Holloway, Richard Maunder, Penelope Cave, pp.26-30
Music Reviews: Richard Maunder, Peter Holloway, pp.30-31
Concert Reviews: Peter Holloway, Richard Maunder, Peter Holloway, pp.32-33
Disc Reviews: Penelope Cave, Richard Leigh Harris, Richard Maunder, Gwilyn Beechey, Tristram Pugin, Peter Holloway, pp.33-44

Harpsichord and fortepiano, x/1 (Autumn 2002)

'A Note from the Editors', Jeremy and Ruth Burbidge, p.2
'An Interview with Stephen Dodgson', Pamela Nash, pp.3-11
'Thomas Morley's Keyboard Music', Gwilyn Beechey, pp.12-15
'Eighteenth Century English Publications of Keyboard Music in the Library of Burghley House, Stamford', Gerald Gifford, pp.16-21
'Tuning the tempérament ordinare', Claudio Di Veroli, pp.22-29
Concert Reviews: Michael Cole, pp.30-31
'Book Reviews: Michael Cole, pp.31-33
Disc Reviews: Penelope Cave, Pamela Nash, Richard Maunder, Richard Leigh Harris, Gwilym Beechey, Peter Watchorn, pp.33-44

Harpsichord and fortepiano, x/2 (Spring 2006)

'A Note from the Editor', Micaela Schmitz, pp.2-3
'Letters', Claire Randall, p.3
'News & Views', pp.3-4
'York Gate Collections: Keyboards', Aaron Shorr, Roy Howat, pp.5-7
'Couperin at the Handel House', Garry Broughton, pp.9-10
'Who's Making/Restoring What?', p.11
'Interview with Dr. Stephen Coles', Kathryn Cok, pp.12-13
'Maintenance: String Replacement', D. J. Law, pp.14-18
'Keyboard Instruments & Quotation: Using a Quotation from C.P.E. Bach', Penelope Cave, pp.19-20
'The Architecture of the Ordres [Couperin]', Jane Clark, pp.21-25
'An Introduction to Restoration Keyboard Music', Terrence Charlston, pp.26-36
'A Quest for Music: Treasures from the University of Leiden Library Revealed, with a Special Focus on Dutch Music 1650-1750', Kathryn Cok, pp.37
'The Clavisimbalum of Henri Arnaut de Zwolle c 1440', Chris Barlow, pp.41-44
'Why is the "Great *In Nomine*" great? [John Bull]', Micaela Schmitz, pp.45-51
Reviews: Micaela Schmitz, Neil Coleman, Penelope Cave, Gerald Gifford, Bridget Cunningham, Giulia Nuti, pp.52-60

Harpsichord and fortepiano, xi/1 [mislabelled Volume 10 No.3 on the cover] (Autumn 2006)

'A Note from the Editor', Micaela Schmitz, p.2
'Letters, News & Views', Susan A. Butt, Davitt Moroney, Paul Thwaites, Hugh Garnett, Jane Clark, Andrew Mayes, pp.3-5
'Conference Report', Anne Beetem Acker, pp.6-9
'Who's Making/Restoring What?', p.10
'Interview with Ton Koopman', Kathryn Cok, pp.11-13
'An Introduction to Restoration Keyboard Music II: Bryne, Roberts and Moss', Terrence Charlston, pp.14-27
'Flamenco Sketches: Part 1 [Scarlatti]', Richard Lester, pp.28-33
'Interpretation on Multiple Keyboards: From the Performer's Perspective', Richard Troeger, pp.34-37
'The Pantalon Clavichord: Resonance from the Eighteenth Century', Paul Simmonds, pp.38-43
'English Upright Grands and Cabinet Pianos', Kenneth Mobbs, pp.44-50
Reviews: David Pickett, Gregory Crowell, Robert Haskins, Beth Garfinkel, Meg Cotner, Patrick Frye III, James McCarty, Callmerio Soares, Penelope Cave, Charlene Brendler, Micaela Schmitz, Madeline Goold, pp.51-63
About our contributors, p.64

Harpsichord and fortepiano, xi/2 (Spring 2007)

'A Note from the Editor', Micaela Schmitz, p.2
'Letters, News & Views', Michael Faulkner, Jane Clark, Anders Henry, David Breitman, pp.3-7
'Conference Report', Gary Carpenter, Judith Conrad, pp.8-11
'Flamenco Sketches: Part 2 [Scarlatti]', Richard Lester, pp.12-16
'The harpsichord in Brazil', Calimerio Soares, pp.17-19
'Mozart and the Clavier', Neil Coleman, pp.20-30 [and see 'Mozart and the Clavier – a Supplement', *HF*, xii/1 (Autumn 2007), pp.30-34]
'Buxtehude's Works for Stringed Keyboard Instruments', John Collins, pp.31-40
'An Overview of Pedal Harpsichord Recordings', Mark Ganullin, pp.41-44
Reviews: Jenny Nex, Rob Haskins, Fabian Mohr, Masumi Yamamoto, Peter Medhurst, Beth Garfinkel, Robin Bigwood, John Weretka, pp.45-53
About our contributors, p.54

Harpsichord and fortepiano, xii/1 [mislabelled Volume 11, No.2 on Index page] (Autumn 2007)

'A Note from the Editor', Micaela Schmitz, p.2
'Letters, News & Views', Michael Faulkner, Jane Clark, pp.3-4
'Conference Report', Anne Beetem Acker, Karen Hite Jacob, Gregory Crowell, Grant Colburn, Gavin Black, John Edwards, pp.5-12
'Who's Making/Restoring What?', p.13
'Interview with Derek Adlam', Paula Woods, pp.14-18
'Interview with Alan Curtis and Bruce Kennedy', Giulia Nuti, pp.19-21
'New Music Focus', Penelope Cave, Bridget Cunningham, Elaine Comparone, Pamela Nash, pp.22-29
'Mozart and the Clavier – a Supplement', Neil Coleman, pp.30-34
Reviews: Richard Troeger, Micaela Schmitz, John Collins, James R. McCarty, Pamela Nash, Douglas Hollick, pp.35-42
About our contributors, p.43

Harpsichord and fortepiano, xii/2 (Spring 2008)

'A Note from the Editor', Micaela Schmitz, p.2
'Letters, News & Views', Jane Clark, Elaine Funaro, pp.3-8
'Obituaries: Joseph Payne, David Bolton, Valda Aveling', pp.5-7
'Who's Making/Restoring What?', p.9
'In Search of Rosenberger [Interviews with Stephen Coles, David Winston and Gary Cooper]', Micaela Schmitz, p.10-14
'Composing *Toccata de Roça* for Solo Harpsichord', Calimerio Soares, pp.15-26
'Scarlatti Sonatas, Step by Step', Penelope Cave, pp.27-29

'Le Clavecin en France', Kasia Tomczak-Feltrin, pp.30-32
'An Approach to Recreating Historical Sound: Part 1', Paul Y. Irvin, pp.33-38
Reviews: John Collins, Bridget Cunningham, Gregory Crowell, Richard Lester, Carol lei Breckenridge, pp.39-43
About our contributors, p.44

Harpsichord and fortepiano, xiii/1 (Autumn 2008)

'A Note from the Editor', Micaela Schmitz, p.2
'Letters, News & Views', Carmelo Bellia, Peter Watchorn, Mimi Waitzman, pp.3-5
'The Once and Future Harpsichord: The Aliénor Competition for Composition', Barbara Norton, pp.6-7
'Who's Making/Restoring What?', p.8
'A Path towards Lid Decoration', Elisabetta Lanzoni, p.9
'Painting Harpsichord Soundboards – my memories', Mary Mobbs, pp.10-16
'Harpsichord Regulation', D. J. Law, pp.17-20
'An Approach to Recreating Historical Sound: Part II', Paul Y. Irvin, pp.21-27
Reviews: Richard Troeger, Micaela Schmitz, John Collins, Gregory Crowell, Steven Devine, David Breitman, Kasia Tomczak-Feltrin, Carol lei Breckenridge, Pamela Hickman, pp.28-39
About our contributors, p.40

Harpsichord and fortepiano, xiii/2 (Spring 2009)

'A Note from the Editor', Micaela Schmitz, pp.2-4
'Letters, News & Views', Gregory Crowell, p.5
'Inside Restoration: An Interview Of Ben Marks and Lucy Coad', pp.6-8
'Who's Making/Restoring What?', p.9
'Frescobaldi Unmasked: Unravelling Complexities of Interpretation within the Toccatas', Richard Lester, pp.10-19
'Thomas Morley's Keyboard Music', Gwilym Beechey, pp.20-23
'Harpsichord Regulation, Part II', D. J. Law, pp.24-27
'Keyboard Temperament in the Nineteenth Century: The Well Tempered Romantic', Daniel Grimwood, pp.28-32
Reviews: Douglas Hollick, Micaela Schmitz, Gregory Crowell, Gerald Gifford, Grant Colburn, Pamela Nash, Kenneth Mobbs, pp.33-40
About our contributors, ibc

Harpsichord and fortepiano, xiv/1 (Autumn 2009)

'A Note from the Editor', Micaela Schmitz, p.2
'Letters, News & Views', David Pinnegar, pp.2-3
'The Atlantis Trio & Ensemble', Peter Watchorn, pp.4-6

'Who's Making/Restoring What?', p.7
'The Bentside Spinets of Stephen Keene and his School', Peter Mole, pp.8-17
'Everything New is Old Again – Part I', Grant Colburn with Micaela Schmitz, pp.18-23
'A Late Florentine Harpsichord Uncovered', Peter Thresh, pp.24-29
Reviews: John Collins, David Breitman, Garry Broughton, Brian Robins, pp.30-41
About our contributors, p.42

Harpsichord and fortepiano, xiv/2 (Spring 2010)

'A Note from the Editor', Micaela Schmitz, p.2
'Letters, News & Views', Peter Watchorn, Emiliano Giannetti, pp.2-3
'Makers' Reports: The Birth of a Harpsichord: Richard Kingston's Opus #333', Caperton Andersson with Richard Kingston, pp.4-5
'Obituary: Owen H. Jorgensen', p.5
'Introduction to the Making of a Pleyel', Paul McNulty, pp.6-7
'Who's Making/Restoring What?', p.8
'"Ziegler Variations": On the Goldberg Polonaises: In Search of the Author', Maxim Serebrennikov, pp.9-15
'Some thoughts on Playing the Goldberg Variations, BWV 988', Richard Leigh Harris, p.16-19
'Everything New is Old Again – Part II', Grant Colburn, Fernando De Luca, Micaela Schmitz, pp.20-29
'Modifying Modern Harpsichord Dampers', Paul Y. Irvin, pp.30-34
Reviews: Grant Colburn, David Pickett, Jacqui Robertson-Wade, Paula Woods, John Collins, Micaela Schmitz, James McCarty, Daniel Goren, pp.35-43
About our contributors, p.44

Harpsichord and fortepiano, xv/1 [mislabelled Volume 14, No.2] (Autumn 2010)

'A Note from the Editor', Micaela Schmitz, p.2
'Letters, News & Views', Colin Booth, Karen Hite Jacob, Barbara King, pp.2-3
'Interview of Myrna Herzog, New Square Piano Owner', Pamela Hickman [with David Shemer], pp.4-5
'Introduction to the Making of a Pleyel (Part II)', Paul McNulty, p.6
'Chopin's Piano Built anew by Chris Maene', p.7
'Who's Making/Restoring What?', p.8
'Valotti as the Ideal German Good Temperament', Claudio Di Veroli, pp.9-14
'A Renaissance Piano?', Christopher Barlow, pp.15-16
'An Overview of the Keyboard Music of Bernardo Pasquini (1637-1710)', John Collins, pp.17-24
'Mattheson's Harmony's Monument: the Twelve Suites of 1714: Clues to the Execution of Rhythm in German Baroque Suites', Colin Booth, pp.25-30 [and see correction in *HF*, xv/2 (Spring 2011), p.3]

Reviews: James McCarty, Micaela Schmitz, Richard Lester, Stefania Neonato, Marcel Zidani, pp.31-36
About our contributors, ibc

Harpsichord and fortepiano, xv/2 (Spring 2011)

'A Note from the Editor', Micaela Schmitz, p.2
'Letters, News & Views', Pamela Nash, Claudio Di Veroli, David Law, pp.2-6
'Reports', Mario S. Tonda, Thomas Bregenzer, pp.7-8
'Obituaries: Martha Novak Clinkscale, Don Angle, Brian Jordan', Douglas Hollick, p.4
'Who's Making/Restoring What?', p.9
'Interview with Bexley Workshops: Maintenance and Tuning Courses [Andrew Wooderson, Edmund Handy]', pp.10-11
'Interview: Maintaining Original Instruments and Allowing Access', Andrew Lamb, pp.12-15
'The Fluid Piano', Christopher Barlow, pp.16-18
'Clavichords, Fretted & Unfretted', Richard Troeger, pp.19-26
'Rudolf Straube', Kah-Ming Ng, pp.27-28
'Interview: Gideon Meir', Pamela Hickman, pp.29-33
Reviews: Jan-Piet Knijff, Calimerio Soares, John Collins, Micaela Schmitz, Pamela Nash, pp.34-40
About our contributors, ibc

Harpsichord and fortepiano, xvi/1 (Autumn 2011)

'A Note from the Editor', Micaela Schmitz, p.2
'Letters, News & Views', Richard Troeger, Damien Mahiet, pp.2-4
'Obituary: Clifford Charles West', David Law, p.3
'Making a Boisselot', Paul McNulty, pp.5-6
'Who's Making/Restoring What?', p.7
'Women of Note', Diana Ambache, pp.8-11
'Elisabeth-Claude Jacquet De La Guerre', Pamela Hickman, pp.12-14
'A Glimpse of the Tagliavini Collection of Musical Instruments', María Virginia Rolfo, pp.15-20
'Book for Thoroughbass (1786) owned by Ms. Avdot'ja Ivanova: Pages from one lady's music album during the period of Catherine the Great', Maxim Serebrennikov, pp.21-26
'Tailoring the Sound of your Keyboard Instrument, Part 1', Paul Y. Irvin, pp.27-32
Reviews: John Collins, Frederic La Croix, Carol lei Breckenridge, Jan-Piet Knijff, Grant Colburn, pp.33-39
About our contributors, p.40

Harpsichord and fortepiano, xvi/2 (Spring 2012)

'A Note from the Editor', Micaela Schmitz, p.2
'Letters, News & Views', pp.2-3
'Jane Austen and the Square Piano', Penelope Cave, pp.4-6
'Who's Making/Restoring What?', p.7
'Optimising Harpsichord Staggering', Claudio Di Veroli, pp.8-13
'Keyboards in Vermillion: with John Koster', pp.14-19
'Tailoring the Sound of your Keyboard Instrument, Part II', Paul Y. Irvin, pp.20-26
'Texture and Playing Style in Classic Keyboard Music', Richard Troeger, pp.27-32
Reviews: Pamela Hickman, Pamela Nash, Douglas Hollick, John Collins,
      John O'Donnell, pp.33-38
About our contributors, p.40

Harpsichord and fortepiano, xvii/1 (Autumn 2012)

'A Note from the Editor', Micaela Schmitz, p.2
'News', pp.2-9
'Obituary: Mary Jeanette Mobbs', pp.5-6
'Who's Making/Restoring What?', p.10
'Rediscovering Clementi's *Gradus ad Parnassum*: A New perspective from the Early
      English Piano', John Khouri, pp.11-14
'Leonhardt the Enigma', Micaela Schmitz, pp.15-21
'To Quill or Not to Quill? [M. R. Levoi and R. P. Williams, Denzil Wraight,
      Tilman Skowroneck]', pp.22-26
Reviews: Brian Robins, Pamela Hickman, John Collins, John O'Donnell,
      Steven Devine, Richard Troeger, Charlene Brendler, pp.27-40
About our contributors, ibc

Harpsichord and fortepiano, xvii/2 (Spring 2013)

'A Note from the Editor', Micaela Schmitz, p.2
'Letters, News & Views', pp.2-4
'Obituary: Dennis Woolley', p.2
'Interview with Tilman Skowroneck', Pamela Hickman, pp.5-11
'Who's Making/Restoring What?', p.12
'Using Appropriate Pitches and Stringing Schedules', Paul Y. Irvin, pp.13-23
'The Oriental Miscellany and the Hindustani Air: "Wild but Pleasing when
      Understood"', Jane Chapman, pp.24-30
'Ten Top Historic Organs', Daniel Moult, pp.31-34
Reviews: Charlene Brendler, Douglas Hollick, Paul Simmonds, pp.35-43
About our contributors, p.44

Harpsichord and fortepiano, xviii/1 (Autumn 2013)

'A Note from the Editor', Micaela Schmitz, p.4
'Letters, News & Views', Douglas Hollick, Rob Brooke, pp.5-7
'Interview with Marina Minkin', Pamela Hickman, pp.8-10
'A Brief Chat with Henk Klop', Micaela Schmitz, p.11
'Who's Making/Restoring What?', p.12
'Interview with Michael Johnson', Paula Woods, pp.13-16
'Tailoring the Sound of your Keyboard Instrument Part IV: Musical Pins', Paul Y. Irvin, pp.17-23
'A Practical Guide to Quilling', John Phillips, pp.24-31
Reviews: John O'Donnell, Brian Robins, Adrian Lenthall, Sergei Istomin, John Collins, Owen Daly, Bruce Reader, pp.32-41
About our contributors, p.42

Harpsichord and fortepiano, xviii/2 (Spring 2014)

'A Note from the Editor', Micaela Schmitz, p.4
'Letters, News & Views', Mark Windisch, Paula Woods, pp.5-8
'Who's Making/Restoring What?', p.9
'Interview with Richard Troeger', pp.10-17
'Interview with Douglas Hollick', Graham Sadler, pp.18-21
'Landowska and the Pleyel pianos: a Foot(pedalled) note to the Harpsichord Revival', Richard Troeger with Elaine Fuller, pp.22-33
Reviews: Pamela Hickman, John Erskine, Adrian Lenthall, Charlene Brendler, John Collins, Richard Lester, Paul Koronka, John Khouri, pp.34-42
About our contributors, p.43

Harpsichord and fortepiano, xix/1 (Autumn 2014)

'A Note from the Editor', Micaela Schmitz, p.4
'Letters, News & Views, pp.4-5
'Copying a 17th-Century French Harpsichord', David Evans, p.6
'Landowska and the Clavichord', Richard Troeger, pp.7-8
'Who's Making/Restoring What?', p.9
'A Tribute to Martin Skowroneck', [Tilman Skowroneck, Richard Ireland, Douglas Amrine, Colin Booth, John Phillips, Alan Curtis], pp.10-16
'C.P.E. Bach at 300', pp.17-21
'Interview with the Editor, Richard Troeger, pp.22-24
'Frans Brüggen Remembered', [Nicola Wemyss], pp.25-29
Reviews: Charlene Brendler, John Collins, Richard Troeger, Pamela Hickman, Jan-Piet Knijff, Bruce Reader, pp.30-42
About our contributors, p.43

Harpsichord and fortepiano, xvix/2 (Spring 2015)

'A Note from the Editor', Micaela Schmitz, p.4
'Letters, News & Views', Angélica Minero Escobar, Paul Simmonds,
    Christopher Stembridge, pp.4-7, 41
About our contributors, p.9
'Christopher Hogwood: The Momument', pp.10-13
'Fingers Crossed: Girolamo Diruta's *Il Transilvano* (1593): A Re-evaluatio',
    Richard Lester, pp.15-26
'Interview with Mahan Esfahani', Pamela Hickman, pp.27-30
'Vermeer's Ruckers Muselar Virginal: Vermeer's Painting of a Ruckers Muselar Virginal
    in *The Music Lesson* c. 1662-65', Dominic Eckersley, pp.31-43

Harpsichord and fortepiano, xx/1 (Autumn 2015)

'A Note from the Editor', Micaela Schmitz, p.4
'Letters, News & Views', Athur Haas, pp.4-5
'Who's Making/Restoring What?', p.6
'Obituary: Ronald Haas', Richard Troeger, p.7
'Vermeer's Ruckers Muselar Virginal: Vermeer's Painting Of A Ruckers Muselar
    Virginal In The Music Lesson c. 1662-65. New Evidence: The Smoking Gun',
    Dominic Eckersley, pp.8-10
'Trills and frills, a variety of inventions: the North Italian art of Diminutione and
    Tremoli', Richard Lester, pp.11-26
'The mid-nineteenth century Pleyel pianos: an appreciation', Richard Troeger, pp.27-38
Reviews: Charlene Brendler, Meg Cotner, Richard Troeger, John Collins, pp.39-42
About our contributors, p.43

Harpsichord and fortepiano, xx/2 (Spring 2016)

'A Note from the Editor', Micaela Schmitz, p.4
'Letters, News & Views; Obituary, Peter Collins', pp.4-6
'Who's Making/Restoring What?', p.7
'Interview with Paul Irvin', Richard Troeger, pp.9-15
'An interview with Maggie Cole', Pamela Hickman, pp.16-21
'The mid-nineteenth century Pleyel pianos: an appreciation, Part II', Richard Troeger,
    pp.22-32
Reviews: John Collins, Charlene Brendler, Richard Troeger, Pamela Hickman,
    Kasia Tomczak-Feltrin, Micaela Schmitz, David Law, pp.32-42
About our contributors, p.43

Harpsichord and fortepiano, xxi/1 (Autumn 2016)

'A Note from the Editor', Micaela Schmitz, p.4
'News', pp.4-6
'Who's Making/Restoring What?', p.7
'Interview with Terence Charlston', Pamela Hickman, pp.8-14
'Registration matters: analyzing Italian Renaissance registration', Richard Lester, pp.15-21
'Unanswered questions: Bach, Forkel, *schellen*, and keyboard touch', Richard Troeger, pp.22-32
Reviews: Richard Troeger, Charlene Brendler, Pamela Nash, Pamela Hickman, pp.33-42
About our contributors, p.43

Harpsichord and fortepiano, xxi/2 (Spring 2017)

'A Note from the Editor', Micaela Schmitz, p.4
'News; Obituaries, Huguette Dreyfus, Gordon Murray; Projects', pp.4-6
'Who's Making/Restoring What?', p.7
'Interview with Michael Tsalka', Pamela Hickman, pp.9-16
'A measured approach to J.S. Bach's Stylus Phantasticus', Claudio Di Veroli, pp.17-26
About our contributors, p.27
'Revisiting keyboard technique', Micaela Schmitz, pp.28-31
Reviews: Richard Troeger, John Collins, Charlene Brendler, pp.32-42

Harpsichord and fortepiano, xxii/1 (Autumn 2017)

'A Note from the Editor', Micaela Schmitz, p.4
'News; Obituary Elisabeth Chojnacka, Zuzana Ružicková', pp.4-7
'A brief account of the Historic Keyboard Society of North America's meeting in Greenville, South Carolina, 25-29 April 2017', Judith Conrad, pp.8-10
'Who's Making/Restoring What?', p.11
'Interview with Kristian Bezuidenhout', Pamela Hickman, pp.12-19
'A triple-strung 17th-century Italian harpsichord', Huw Saunders, pp.20-27
'Chambonnières versus Louis Couperin: attributing the F major Chaconne', Francis Knights, Pablo Padilla and Dan Tidhar, pp.28-32
Reviews: Micaela Schmitz, John Collins, Charlene Brendler, Pamela Hickman, Micaela Schmitz, Kathryn Cok, Pamela Hickman, pp.33-41
About our contributors, p.42

Harpsichord and fortepiano, xxii/2 (Spring 2018)

'A Note from the Editor', Micaela Schmitz, p.4
'News', pp.4-6
'Obituary: Kenneth Mobbs 1925-2017', pp.7-9
'Who's Making/Restoring What?', p.10
'Interview with Jory Vinikour', Pamela Hickman, pp.12-19
'Fortepiano-harpsichord duos in two eighteenth-century salons', Rebecca Cypess, pp.20-25
'Interview Jane Clark Dodgson in her 90th year', Pamela Nash, pp.26-31
Reviews: Kathryn Cok, Charlene Brendler, Pamela Hickman, John Collins, Micaela Schmitz, pp.32-40
About our contributors, p.42

Harpsichord and fortepiano, xxiii/1 (Autumn 2018)

'A Note from the Editor', Micaela Schmitz, p.4
'News', pp.4-6
'New WAAPA Collection', pp.7-8
'Who's Making/Restoring What?', p.9
'Heather Slade-Lipkin (1947-2017): Harpsichord Pioneer', Pamela Nash, pp.10-15
'Accurate meantone tuning based on Fogliano', Claudio Di Veroli, pp.16-20
'Learning 'The 48'', Francis Knights, pp.21-31
Reviews: John Collins, Micaela Schmitz, Kathryn Cok, Pamela Hickman, pp.32-37
About our contributors, p.38

Harpsichord and fortepiano, xxiii/2 (Spring 2019)

'A Note from the Editor', Micaela Schmitz, p.4
'Letters, News and Views including obituary for Wolfgang Zuckermann', pp.4-6
'Couperin Conference Report', pp.6-7
About our contributors, p.8
'Who's Making/Restoring What?', p.9
'Interview with Robert Levin', Pamela Nash, pp.10-12
'David Evans 1963 [recte 1936]-2018: An Appreciation', Terence Charlston, pp.13-18
'Women in Early Music: Interview with Pamela Nash; Interview with Emer Buckley; Interview with Medea Bindewald', pp.19-26
'Baroque Keyboard Fingering and Present-Day Practice', Claudio Di Veroli, pp.27-34
Reviews: John Collins, Pamela Hickman, Meg Cotner, pp.35-38

Harpsichord & fortepiano, xxiv/1 (Autumn 2019)

'"Because they could never have equaled their father in his style": creativity at the
    keyboard in the Bach family', David Schulenberg, pp.4-7
'The Current State of Claviorgan Research', Eleanor Smith, pp.8-11
'Varied Dispositions', Richard Troeger, pp.12-17
'Couperin's *Misterieuse* Fourth Harpsichord Book', Pieter Dirksen, pp.18-23
'Interview: Orhan Memed', Francis Knights, pp.24-26
Reviews: Francis Knights, John Collins, Meg Cotner, Charlene Brendler,
    Pamela Hickman, pp.27-33
Reports: Francis Knights, David Pinnegar, Anna Maria McElwain, pp.34-35
News and events, pp.36-39

Harpsichord & fortepiano, xxiv/2 (Spring 2020)

'The harpsichord in 19th-century England', Peter Holman, pp.4-14
'Performing François Couperin's *Les Baricades Mistérieuses*', Claudio di Veroli, pp.15-19
'Recording the Fitzwilliam Virginal Book', Pieter-Jan Belder, pp.20-23
'Composer anniversaries in 2020', John Collins, pp.24-27
'Interview: Christoph Hammer', Pamela Hickman, pp.28-31
'The musician's bookshelf: J. S. Bach', Francis Knights, p.32
Reviews: Douglas Hollick, David Ponsford, Paula Woods, John Collins, Francis Knights,
    Pablo Padilla, Pamela Hickman, Ivan Moody, pp.33-41
News and Obituaries, pp.42-43
Correspondence: Paul Simmonds, p.43

Harpsichord & fortepiano, xxv/1 (Autumn 2020)

'Bach on the harpsichord – some personal reflections'. Colin Booth, pp.4-10
'The *Clavecin Roïal* and the first copy in modern times', Kerstin Schwarz, pp.11-14
'The challenges of a modern recording on a Pleyel harpsichord', Christopher D. Lewis,
    pp.15-20
'Remembering Joan Benson', Peter Brownlee, pp.21-27
'Interview with Richard Taylor', Paula Woods, pp.28-30
Reviews: Penelope Cave, Francis Knights, John Collins, John Kitchen, Pamela Hickman,
    pp.31-38
Reports: Anne Beetem Acker, Liselotte Sels, pp.39-40
News and events, pp.40-43

Harpsichord & fortepiano, xxv/2 (Spring 2021)

'"Queen Elizabeth's Virginals": from Venice to the Victoria & Albert Museum',
    Catherine Lorigan, pp.4-13
'The keyboard music of Charles Burney', Francis Knights, pp.13-23
'Muzio Clementi's contribution to the history of music', Marina Rodríguez Brià, pp.24-27
'Composer Anniversaries 2021', John Collins, pp.28-31
'Remembering Kenneth Gilbert', Andrew Appel, pp.32-34
'A commemoration of Elizabeth de la Porte', Pamela Nash, pp.35-36
'Interview with Carole Cerasi', Pamela Hickman, pp.37-40
Reviews: Margaret Debenham, Michael Graham, Penelope Cave, Francis Knights,
    David Griffel, Jon Baxendale, John Kitchen, Kathryn Cok, Pamela Hickman,
    pp.41-49
Correspondence: Paul Simmonds, p.50
News and events, p.51

Harpsichord & fortepiano, xxvi/1 (Autumn 2021)

'Portuguese keyboard music from the second half of the 18th century',
    Mafalda Nejmeddine, pp.4-8
'Flamenco sketches (revisited)', Richard Lester, pp.9-15
'Controlling dynamics on the harpsichord: some examples of techniques employed by
    18th-century composers', Colin Booth, pp.16-20
'Keyboard instruments – some collective thoughts', Paul Simmonds, pp.21-28
'"An Eagle over Falcons": recording harpsichord music by John Worgan (1724-1790)',
    Julian Perkins, pp.29-30
'Early keyboard technology instruction in the US', Allan Winkler, pp.21-32
Reviews: Penelope Cave, Francis Knights, Pablo Padilla, Christopher Kent,
    John Kitchen, David Griffel, pp.33-38
News and events, p.39

Harpsichord & fortepiano, xxvi/2 (Spring 2022)

'"Eloquent Fingers": indications and implications of fingering in Sweelinck's keyboard
    music', Kathryn Cok, pp.4-9
'Harpsichords in Bach's Germany: an overview', Leonard Schick, pp.10-20
'1741: three masterworks of diversity', Claudio Di Veroli, pp.21-26
'William Babell's recently discovered toccatas', Andrew Woolley, pp.27-30
'Composer anniversaries in 2022', John Collins, pp.31-34
'Interview with Richard Lester', Paula Woods, pp.35-38
Reviews: Francis Knights, John Collins, Christopher Kent, John Irving, Luke Mitchell,
    Jon Baxendale, pp.39-47
News and events, p.47

Harpsichord & fortepiano, xxvii/1 (Autumn 2022)

'Claudio Merulo: Two biographical notes', Glen Wilson, pp.4-10
'The *Orgelbüchlein* as pedal clavichord music', Terence Charlston, pp.11-15
'Identifying clavichord repertoire', Paul Simmonds, pp.16-22
'Ivory Sales in the United Kingdom and European Community', David Hackett,
    pp.23-24
'Interview with Andreas Kilström', Hila Katz, pp.25-28
Reviews: Francis Knights, John Collins, Terence Charlston, Michael Maxwell Steer,
    Pablo Padilla, Paula Woods, Pamela Hickman, pp.29-37
Reports, Kathryn Cok, Dylan L. Sanzenbacher, pp.38-40
News and events, pp.40-43

Harpsichord & fortepiano, xxvii/2 (Spring 2023)

'Michael Thomas (1922–2022): a centenary tribute', Thomas McGeary, pp.4-11
'Forkel's Bach revisited', Claudio Di Veroli, pp.12-19
'Clavichords at Vassar College', Laurence Libin, pp.20-25
'An unusual square piano "ravalement"', Paul Simmonds, pp.26-30
'Composer Anniversaries in 2023', John Collins, pp.31-33
'Remembering Malcolm Rose (1948-2022)', Paul Simmonds, pp.34-35
Reviews: Francis Knights, John Collins, Thomas Allery, Pablo Padilla, Pierre Riley,
    pp.36-40
Listings, pp.41-43

Harpsichord & fortepiano, xxviii/1 (Autumn 2023) - *50th Anniversary issue*

'50 years of *Harpsichord & Fortepiano*', Francis Knights, pp.4-7
'Bach at the keyboard: The organist at home', Colin Booth, pp.8-14
'Restoring the 'golden' harpsichord', John R. Bell, pp.15-18
'Modern vs historical harpsichord plucking', Paul Y. Irvin, pp.19-21
'In the Beginning was the Harpsichord', John Koster, pp.22-25
'A perspective on historical keyboard playing in the UK', Terence Charlston, pp.26-27
'Music and criticism: Revisiting George Malcolm's thoughts on authenticity',
    Richard Lester, pp.28-30
'Clavichord gatherings', Richard Troeger, pp.31-34
'Swimming upstream: Reflections of an American harpsichordist from across "The
    Pond"', Mark Kroll, pp.35-38
'The venerable "Boalch" - ready for its next 70 years', John Watson, pp.39-41
'Full Circle? Observations on keyboard music to c.1630 in Musica Britannica and some
    thoughts about the future', David J. Smith, pp.42-44
'Interview with harpsichord maker Milan Misina', Pamela Nash, pp.45-47

SUBJECT INDEX

This is a list of articles by subject, arranged either by date of publication or (where names are included) alphabetically. It does not include details of Reviews: reports, editorials, news, letters or music supplements, details of which can be found in the Main Index, p.3.

1. INSTRUMENTS

1.1 Medieval Keyboard Instruments

'The Musical Mechanisms of Arnaut de Zwolle', John Lester, *The English Harpsichord Magazine*, iii/3 (October 1982), pp.35-41

'An Early Clavycytherium Reconstructed', Peter Bavington, *The English Harpsichord Magazine*, iii/6 (April 1984), pp.106-111

'The Clavisimbalum of Henri Arnaut de Zwolle c 1440', Chris Barlow, *Harpsichord and fortepiano*, x/2 (Spring 2006), pp.41-44

'A Renaissance Piano?', Christopher Barlow, *Harpsichord and fortepiano*, xv/1 (Autumn 2010), pp.15-16

1.2 Virginals & Spinet

'The English Virginals: I', Richard Luckett, *The English Harpsichord Magazine*, i/3 (October 1974), pp.69-72

'The Virginal at the Museum of London', Edgar Hunt, *The English Harpsichord Magazine*, iii/4 (April 1983), p.79

'Musings on the Muselar', Edgar Hunt, *The (English) Harpsichord Magazine*, iii/7 (October 1984), pp.143-144

'The Bentside Spinets of Stephen Keene and his School', Peter Mole, *Harpsichord and fortepiano*, xiv/1 (Autumn 2009), pp.8-17

'Vermeer's Ruckers Muselar Virginal: Vermeer's Painting of a Ruckers Muselar Virginal in *The Music Lesson* c. 1662-65', Dominic Eckersley, *Harpsichord and fortepiano*, xvix/2 (Spring 2015), pp.31-43

'Vermeer's Ruckers Muselar Virginal: Vermeer's Painting Of A Ruckers Muselar Virginal In The Music Lesson c. 1662-65. New Evidence: The Smoking Gun', Dominic Eckersley, *Harpsichord and fortepiano*, xx/1 (Autumn 2015), pp.8-10

'"Queen Elizabeth's Virginals": from Venice to the Victoria & Albert Museum', Catherine Lorigan, *Harpsichord & fortepiano*, xxv/2 (Spring 2021), pp.4-13

1.3 Clavichord

'The Fretted Clavichord', Michael Thomas, *The English Harpsichord Magazine*, i/2 (April 1974), pp.39-47

'The Tunings and Pitch of Early Clavichords', *The English Harpsichord Magazine*, i/6 (April 1976), Michael Thomas, pp.175-180

'The Fretted Clavichord', Michael Thomas, *The English Harpsichord Magazine*, iv/2 (1986), pp.33-44

'The Pantalon Clavichord: Resonance from the Eighteenth Century', Paul Simmonds, *Harpsichord and fortepiano*, xi/1 (Autumn 2006), pp.38-43

'Mozart and the Clavier', Neil Coleman, *Harpsichord and fortepiano*, xi/2 (Spring 2007), pp.20-30

'Mozart and the Clavier – a Supplement', Neil Coleman, *Harpsichord and fortepiano*, xii/1 (Autumn 2007), pp.30-34

'Clavichords, Fretted & Unfretted', Richard Troeger, *Harpsichord and fortepiano*, xv/2 (Spring 2011), pp.19-26

'Landowska and the Clavichord', Richard Troeger, *Harpsichord and fortepiano*, xix/1 (Autumn 2014), pp.7-8

'Keyboard instruments – some collective thoughts', Paul Simmonds, *Harpsichord & fortepiano*, xxvi/1 (Autumn 2021), pp.21-28

'The *Orgelbüchlein* as pedal clavichord music', Terence Charlston, *Harpsichord & fortepiano*, xxvii/1 (Autumn 2022), pp.11-15

'Identifying clavichord repertoire', Paul Simmonds, *Harpsichord & fortepiano*, xxvii/1 (Autumn 2022), pp.16-22

'Clavichords at Vassar College', Laurence Libin, *Harpsichord & fortepiano*, xxvii/2 (Spring 2023), pp.20-25

'Clavichord gatherings', Richard Troeger, *Harpsichord & fortepiano*, xxviii/1 (Autumn 2023), pp.31-34

1.4 Organ

'Organ Restoration in Florence, Rudolph Kremer, *The English Harpsichord Magazine*, ii/2 (April 1978), pp.37-39

'Two small Organs revived', L. A. Esteves Pereria, *The English Harpsichord Magazine*, iii/4 (April 1983), pp.73-76

'Organs of Upper Austria', *The (English) Harpsichord Magazine*, iii/8 (April 1985), p.154

'Ten Top Historic Organs', Daniel Moult, *Harpsichord and fortepiano*, xvii/2 (Spring 2013), pp.31-34

'Registration matters: analyzing Italian Renaissance registration', Richard Lester, *Harpsichord and fortepiano*, xxi/1 (Autumn 2016), pp.15-21

1.5 Fortepiano & Early Piano

'An Interesting Early Forte-Piano', C. F. Colt, *The English Harpsichord Magazine*, i/7 (October 1976), pp.198-201

'A Forte-piano at the Instrumental Museum – Lisbon', L. A. Esteves Pereria, *The English Harpsichord Magazine*, iii/4 (April 1983), pp.67-70

'Playing Mozart On The Fortepiano', Christopher Kite, *The Harpsichord and Fortepiano Magazine*, iv/3 (April 1987), pp.52-55

'Americus Backers: Original Forte Piano Maker', Warwick Henry Cole, *The Harpsichord and Fortepiano Magazine*, iv/4 (October 1987), pp.79-85

'On the New Fortepiano in Contemporary German Musical Writings', Katalin Komlos, *The Harpsichord and Fortepiano Magazine*, iv/6 (October 1988), pp.134-139

'*Philibuster*: New music for the fortepiano', Marc Reichow and Richard Sims, *Harpsichord and fortepiano*, v/3 (October 1995), pp.23-29

'Fortepiano kapsels old and new', Martha Goodway, *Harpsichord and fortepiano*, vi/1 (May 1997), pp.13-16

'English Upright Grands and Cabinet Pianos', Kenneth Mobbs, *Harpsichord and fortepiano*, xi/1 (Autumn 2006), pp.44-50

'In Search of Rosenberger [Interviews with Stephen Coles, David Winston and Gary Cooper]', Micaela Schmitz, *Harpsichord and fortepiano*, xii/2 (Spring 2008), p.10-14

'A Renaissance Piano?', Christopher Barlow, *Harpsichord and fortepiano*, xv/1 (Autumn 2010), pp.15-16

'Fortepiano-harpsichord duos in two eighteenth-century salons', Rebecca Cypess, *Harpsichord and fortepiano*, xxii/2 (Spring 2018), pp.20-25

'The *Clavecin Roïal* and the first copy in modern times', Kerstin Schwarz, *Harpsichord & fortepiano*, xxv/1 (Autumn 2020), pp.11-14

'An unusual square piano "ravalement"', Paul Simmonds, *Harpsichord & fortepiano*, xxvii/2 (Spring 2023), pp.26-30

1.6 19th century Pianos

'Dussek, Broadwood and the Additional Keys', Mora Carroll, *Harpsichord and fortepiano*, viii/1 (Autumn 1999), pp.3-10

'Jan Ladislav Dussek and his music for the extended keyboard compass', Mora Carroll, *Harpsichord and fortepiano*, ix/2 (Summer 2001), pp.8-15

'Introduction to the Making of a Pleyel', Paul McNulty, *Harpsichord and fortepiano*, xiv/2 (Spring 2010), pp.6-7

'Introduction to the Making of a Pleyel (Part II)', Paul McNulty, *Harpsichord and fortepiano*, xv/1 (Autumn 2010), p.6

'Chopin's Piano Built anew by Chris Maene', *Harpsichord and fortepiano*, xv/1 (Autumn 2010), p.7

'Jane Austen and the Square Piano', Penelope Cave, *Harpsichord and fortepiano*, xvi/2 (Spring 2012), pp.4-6

'Landowska and the Pleyel pianos: a Foot(pedalled) note to the Harpsichord Revival', Richard Troeger with Elaine Fuller, *Harpsichord and fortepiano*, xviii/2 (Spring 2014), pp.22-33

'The mid-nineteenth century Pleyel pianos: an appreciation', Richard Troeger, *Harpsichord and fortepiano*, xx/1 (Autumn 2015), pp.27-38

'The mid-nineteenth century Pleyel pianos: an appreciation, Part II', Richard Troeger, *Harpsichord and fortepiano*, xx/2 (Spring 2016), pp.22-32

'Making a Boisselot', Paul McNulty, *Harpsichord and fortepiano*, xvi/1 (Autumn 2011), pp.5-6

1.7 Other Keyboard Instruments

'The Archicembalo of Nicola Vincentino', Marco Tiella, *The English Harpsichord Magazine*, i/5 (October 1975), pp.134-144

'The Claviorganum in England', Stephen Wessel, *The English Harpsichord Magazine*, i/8 (April 1977), pp.226-233

'An Octave Harpsichord at the Instrumental Museum - Lisbon', L. A. Esteves Pereira, *The English Harpsichord Magazine*, ii/2 (April 1978), pp.30-32

'The Upright Harpsichord', Michael Thomas, *The English Harpsichord Magazine*, ii/4 (April 1979), pp.84-92

'A Modern Upright Harpsichord', John Paul, *The English Harpsichord Magazine*, ii/5 (October 1979), pp.124-125

'An Early Clavycytherium Reconstructed', Peter Bavington, *The English Harpsichord Magazine*, iii/6 (April 1984), pp.106-111

'The Pedal Harpsichord – A Recent Reconstruction', Colin Booth, *The Harpsichord and Fortepiano Magazine*, iv/5 (April 1988), pp.117-120

'The Clavisimbalum of Henri Arnaut de Zwolle c 1440', Chris Barlow, *Harpsichord and fortepiano*, x/2 (Spring 2006), pp.41-44

'An Overview of Pedal Harpsichord Recordings', Mark Ganullin, *Harpsichord and fortepiano*, xi/2 (Spring 2007), pp.41-44

'A Renaissance Piano?', Christopher Barlow, *Harpsichord and fortepiano*, xv/1 (Autumn 2010), pp.15-16

'The Fluid Piano', Christopher Barlow, *Harpsichord and fortepiano*, xv/2 (Spring 2011), pp.16-18

'The Current State of Claviorgan Research', Eleanor Smith, *Harpsichord & fortepiano*, xxiv/1 (Autumn 2019), pp.8-11

'The *Clavecin Roïal* and the first copy in modern times', Kerstin Schwarz, *Harpsichord & fortepiano*, xxv/1 (Autumn 2020), pp.11-14

'In the Beginning was the Harpsichord', John Koster, *Harpsichord & fortepiano*, xxviii/1 (Autumn 2023), pp.22-25

1.8 Restoration and Conservation

'Organ Restoration in Florence', Rudolph Kremer, *The English Harpsichord Magazine*, ii/2 (April 1978), pp.37-39

'Thoughts on the Restoration of Harpsichords', Michael Thomas, *The English Harpsichord Magazine*, ii/3 (October 1978), pp.62-67

'Recent Harpsichord Restorations (I)', Michael Thomas, *The English Harpsichord Magazine*, iii/3 (October 1982), pp.45-48

'Recent Harpsichord Restorations (II)', Michael Thomas, *The English Harpsichord Magazine*, iii/4 (April 1983), pp.71-72, 79

'Conservation conversation', Mimi Waitzman, *Harpsichord and fortepiano*, v/1 (October 1994), p.26

'A Bone of Contention: Should we stop restoring and playing original instruments?', Göran Grahn, *Harpsichord and fortepiano*, v/1 (October 1994), pp.27-28

'…Or should good restoration still be carried out?', David Winston, *Harpsichord and fortepiano*, v/1 (October 1994), p.29

'Restoring the 'golden' harpsichord', John R. Bell, *Harpsichord & fortepiano*, xxviii/1 (Autumn 2023), pp.15-18

2. KEYBOARDS and MAKERS

2.1 Great Britain

'Early English Harpsichord Building: A Reassessment', Thomas McGeary, *The Harpsichord Magazine*, i/1 (October 1973), pp.7-19, 30

'The Broadwood Books: I', Charles Mould, *The Harpsichord Magazine*, i/1 (October 1973), pp.19-23

'An Early-Eighteenth-century Harpsichord by Thomas Barton', Charles Mould, *The English Harpsichord Magazine*, i/2 (April 1974), pp.36-38

'The English Virginals: I', Richard Luckett, *The English Harpsichord Magazine*, i/3 (October 1974), pp.69-72

'The Claviorganum in England', Stephen Wessel, *The English Harpsichord Magazine*, i/8 (April 1977), pp.226-233

'Master Brian his Virginall [Lodewijk Theeuwes]', Brian Morgan, *The English Harpsichord Magazine*, ii/5 (October 1979), pp.114-115

'The Virginal at the Museum of London', Edgar Hunt, *The English Harpsichord Magazine*, iii/4 (April 1983), p.79

'Another Burkat Tchudi Harpichord Found', L. A. Esteves Pereria, *The English Harpsichord Magazine*, iii/6 (April 1984), p.119

'Americus Backers: Original Forte Piano Maker', Warwick Henry Cole, *The Harpsichord and Fortepiano Magazine*, iv/4 (October 1987), pp.79-85

'The harpsichord in 19th-century England', Peter Holman, *Harpsichord & fortepiano*, xxiv/2 (Spring 2020), pp.4-14

2.2 Flanders

'Master Brian his Virginall [Lodewijk Theeuwes]', Brian Morgan, *The English Harpsichord Magazine*, ii/5 (October 1979), pp.114-115

'The Haward Harpsichord at Knole', Dennis Woolley, *The English Harpsichord Magazine*, iii/1 (October 1981), pp.2-3

'Musings on the Muselar', Edgar Hunt, *The (English) Harpsichord Magazine*, iii/7 (October 1984), pp.143-144

'Windebank's Virginall: A Lost Ruckers Harpsichord', Paula Woods, *Harpsichord and fortepiano*, ix/1 (Spring 2001), pp.16-23

'Vermeer's Ruckers Muselar Virginal: Vermeer's Painting of a Ruckers Muselar Virginal in *The Music Lesson* c. 1662-65', Dominic Eckersley, *Harpsichord and fortepiano*, xvix/2 (Spring 2015), pp.31-43

'Vermeer's Ruckers Muselar Virginal: Vermeer's Painting Of A Ruckers Muselar Virginal In The Music Lesson c. 1662-65. New Evidence: The Smoking Gun', Dominic Eckersley, *Harpsichord and fortepiano*, xx/1 (Autumn 2015), pp.8-10

'Restoring the 'golden' harpsichord', John R. Bell, *Harpsichord & fortepiano*, xxviii/1 (Autumn 2023), pp.15-18

2.3 Italy

'Venetian Harpsichords', Michael Thomas, *The English Harpsichord Magazine*, i/4 (April 1975), pp.109-120

'The Archicembalo of Nicola Vincentino', Marco Tiella, *The English Harpsichord Magazine*, i/5 (October 1975), pp.134-144

'The Development of the Tuning and Tone Colour of an Instrument made in Venice about 1500', Michael Thomas, *The English Harpsichord Magazine*, i/5 (October 1975), pp.145-155

'Two Harpsichords by Elpidio Gregori', William Dow, *The Harpsichord and Fortepiano Magazine*, iv/6 (October 1988), pp.140-145

'Ligurian harpsichord investigated', Maurizio Tarrini, *Harpsichord and fortepiano*, v/2 (April 1995), pp.33-34

'The 1531 Trasuntino Harpsichord in a Universal European Pitch System', Nicholas Mitchell, *Harpsichord and fortepiano*, ix/1 (Spring 2001), pp.7-13

'A Late Florentine Harpsichord Uncovered', Peter Thresh, *Harpsichord and fortepiano*, xiv/1 (Autumn 2009), pp.24-29

'A triple-strung 17th-century Italian harpsichord', Huw Saunders, *Harpsichord and fortepiano*, xxii/1 (Autumn 2017), pp.20-27

2.4 France

'Early French Harpsichords', Michael Thomas, *The English Harpsichord Magazine*, i/3 (October 1974), pp.73-84

'Harpsichords which have been found recently in France', Michael Thomas, *The English Harpsichord Magazine*, ii/7 (October 1980), pp.158-163

'A Seventeenth Century French Harpsichord', Chris Nobbs, *The Harpsichord and Fortepiano Magazine*, iv/3 (April 1987), pp.46-51 [see also *HF* iv/4 (October 1987), pp.102-103]

'A Seventeenth Century French Harpsichord?', Chris Nobbs, *The Harpsichord and Fortepiano Magazine*, iv/4 (October 1987), pp.102-103

'Copying a 17th-Century French Harpsichord', David Evans, *Harpsichord and fortepiano*, xix/1 (Autumn 2014), p.6

2.5 Germany & Austria

'The Hudiksvall Mietke', Andreas Kilström, *Harpsichord and fortepiano*, v/1 (October 1994), pp.15-18

'Keyboard Instruments in Haydn's Vienna', Richard Maunder, *Harpsichord and fortepiano*, vii/1 (June 1998), pp.5-10

'Varied Dispositions', Richard Troeger, *Harpsichord & fortepiano*, xxiv/1 (Autumn 2019), pp.12-17

'The *Clavecin Roïal* and the first copy in modern times', Kerstin Schwarz, *Harpsichord & fortepiano*, xxv/1 (Autumn 2020), pp.11-14

'Harpsichords in Bach's Germany: an overview', Leonard Schick, *Harpsichord & fortepiano*, xxvi/2 (Spring 2022), pp.10-20

2.6 Other Countries

'The Harpsichord at the Courtauld Institute', *The English Harpsichord Magazine*, i/7 (October 1976), Michael Thomas, pp.194-197

'A Harpsichord from Switzerland', Will Bruggmann, *The English Harpsichord Magazine*, ii/2 (April 1978), pp.40-44

'Early keyboards in Argentina', Claudio Di Veroli, *Harpsichord and fortepiano*, vi/2 (November 1997), pp.20-21

2.6 Modern Keyboard Makers

'Harpsichord Construction in Canada', Barry Ainslie, *The English Harpsichord Magazine*, ii/3 (October 1978), pp.58-62

'The Pleyel Harpsichord', J. A. Richard, *The English Harpsichord Magazine*, ii/5 (October 1979), pp.110-113

'A Modern Upright Harpsichord', John Paul, *The English Harpsichord Magazine*, ii/5 (October 1979), pp.124-125

'Makers' Reports: The Birth of a Harpsichord: Richard Kingston's Opus #333', Caperton Andersson with Richard Kingston, *Harpsichord and fortepiano*, xiv/2 (Spring 2010), pp.4-5

'Copying a 17th-Century French Harpsichord', David Evans, *Harpsichord and fortepiano*, xix/1 (Autumn 2014), p.6

'The challenges of a modern recording on a Pleyel harpsichord', Christopher D. Lewis, *Harpsichord & fortepiano*, xxv/1 (Autumn 2020), pp.15-20

'Clavichords at Vassar College', Laurence Libin, *Harpsichord & fortepiano*, xxvii/2 (Spring 2023), pp.20-25

2.7 Instrument Selection

'On choosing a Harpsichord', Edgar Hunt, *The English Harpsichord Magazine*, iii/5 (October 1983), pp.97-98

'Keyboard Instruments in Haydn's Vienna', Richard Maunder, *Harpsichord and fortepiano*, vii/1 (June 1998), pp.5-10

'Interpretation on Multiple Keyboards: From the Performer's Perspective', Richard Troeger, *Harpsichord and fortepiano*, xi/1 (Autumn 2006), pp.34-37

'Mozart and the Clavier', Neil Coleman, *Harpsichord and fortepiano*, xi/2 (Spring 2007), pp.20-30

'Mozart and the Clavier – a Supplement', Neil Coleman, *Harpsichord and fortepiano*, xii/1 (Autumn 2007), pp.30-34

2.8 Decoration

'"Take Six Eggs…": Making and using egg tempera on harpsichord soundboards', Jenny Haylett, *Harpsichord and fortepiano*, v/2 (April 1995), pp.20-22

'Soundboard painting: The Traditional Touch', Mary Mobbs, *Harpsichord and fortepiano*, v/3 (October 1995), pp.31-32

'A Path towards Lid Decoration', Elisabetta Lanzoni, *Harpsichord and fortepiano*, xiii/1 (Autumn 2008), p.9

'Painting Harpsichord Soundboards – my memories', Mary Mobbs, *Harpsichord and fortepiano*, xiii/1 (Autumn 2008), pp.10-16

'Ivory Sales in the United Kingdom and European Community', David Hackett, *Harpsichord & fortepiano*, xxvii/1 (Autumn 2022), pp.23-24

3. STRINGING, TUNING and MAINTENANCE

3.1 Stringing and Pitch

'Early Eighteenth-Century English Harpsichord Tuning and Stringing', Thomas McGeary, *The English Harpsichord Magazine*, iii/2 (April 1982), pp.18-22

'Harpsichords…with all the different-siz'd wire used in that instrument (I)', J. J. K. Rhodes and W. R. Thomas, *The English Harpsichord Magazine*, iii/6 (April 1984), pp.116-118

'Harpsichords…with all the different-siz'd wire used in that instrument (II)', J. J. K. Rhodes and W. R. Thomas, *The (English) Harpsichord Magazine*, iii/7 (October 1984), pp.130-133

'Harpsichords…with all the different-siz'd wire used in that instrument (III)', J. J. K. Rhodes and W. R. Thomas, *The (English) Harpsichord Magazine*, iii/8 (April 1985), pp.152-154

'The 1531 Trasuntino Harpsichord in a Universal European Pitch System', Nicholas Mitchell, *Harpsichord and fortepiano*, ix/1 (Spring 2001), pp.7-13

'Using Appropriate Pitches and Stringing Schedules', Paul Y. Irvin, *Harpsichord and fortepiano*, xvii/2 (Spring 2013), pp.13-23

3.2 Tuning and Temperament

'Tuning and Temperament', Edgar Hunt, *The English Harpsichord Magazine*, i/7 (October 1976), pp.201-204

'Tuning and Temperaments', Roy Truby, *The English Harpsichord Magazine*, i/8 (April 1977), p.235

'Tuning Systems for 12-note Keyboard Instruments', Mark Lindley, *The English Harpsichord Magazine*, ii/1 (October 1977), pp.13-15

'Early Eighteenth-Century English Harpsichord Tuning and Stringing', Thomas McGeary, *The English Harpsichord Magazine*, iii/2 (April 1982), pp.18-22

'Is there an Enigma in Werckmeister's "Musicalische Temperatur"?', Herbert Anton Kellner, *The (English) Harpsichord Magazine*, iii/7 (October 1984), pp.134-136

'One typographical Enigma in Werckmeister, "Musicalische Temperatur"', Herbert Anton Kellner, *The (English) Harpsichord Magazine*, iii/8 (April 1985), pp.146-151

'Did Werckmeister already know the tuning of J. S. Bach for the "48"?', Herbert Anton Kellner, *The (English) Harpsichord Magazine*, iv/1 (October 1985), pp.7-11

'The temperament for Bach's "48"', Michael Thomas, *The English Harpsichord Magazine*, iv/2 (1986), pp.18-21

'How Bach quantified his well-tempered tuning within the FOUR DUETS', Herbert Anton Kellner, *The English Harpsichord Magazine*, iv/2 (1986), pp.21-27

'PitchMan: Budget-priced electronic tuner for historical temperaments', Dave Gayman, *Harpsichord and fortepiano*, v/3 (October 1995), pp.11-14

'The Cent System: with an easy method of calculation', Carl Sloane, *Harpsichord and fortepiano*, v/3 (October 1995), pp.15-16

'Mean as they come: Clues in the elucidation of Handel's harpsichord temperament', Carl Sloane, *Harpsichord and fortepiano*, v/3 (October 1995), pp.17-19

'Handel's Temperament – A Revised View', Carl Sloane, *Harpsichord and fortepiano*, vi/2 (November 1997), p.35

'Tuning the tempérament ordinare', Claudio Di Veroli, *Harpsichord and fortepiano*, x/1 (Autumn 2002), pp.22-29

'Keyboard Temperament in the Nineteenth Century: The Well Tempered Romantic', Daniel Grimwood, *Harpsichord and fortepiano*, xiii/2 (Spring 2009), pp.28-32

'Valotti as the Ideal German Good Temperament', Claudio Di Veroli, *Harpsichord and fortepiano*, xv/1 (Autumn 2010), pp.9-14

'Accurate meantone tuning based on Fogliano', Claudio Di Veroli, *Harpsichord and fortepiano*, xxiii/1 (Autumn 2018), pp.16-20

3.3 Maintenance

'Harpsichord Building: I. Preparing the Action for Voicing', Dave Law, *The Harpsichord Magazine*, i/1 (October 1973), pp.23-25

'Harpsichord Building: II. Voicing and Regulating', Dave Law, *The English Harpsichord Magazine*, i/2 (April 1974), pp.53-57

'Harpsichord Building: Preparing the Action for Voicing', Dave Law, *The English Harpsichord Magazine*, iii/5 (October 1983), pp.98-102, 96

'Care of…: Regular maintenance of your keyboard', Mimi Waitzman, *Harpsichord and fortepiano*, v/1 (October 1994), pp.41-42

'Care of…: Regular maintenance of your keyboard', Mimi Waitzman, *Harpsichord and fortepiano*, v/2 (April 1995), pp.40-41

'Care of…: Regular maintenance of your keyboard', Mimi Waitzman, *Harpsichord and fortepiano*, v/3 (October 1995), pp.38-39

'The vital rôle of humidity', Martin Robertson, *Harpsichord and fortepiano*, vi/1 (May 1997), p.27

'Maintenance: String Replacement', D. J. Law, *Harpsichord and fortepiano*, x/2 (Spring 2006), pp.14-18

'Harpsichord Regulation', D. J. Law, *Harpsichord and fortepiano*, xiii/1 (Autumn 2008), pp.17-20

'Harpsichord Regulation, Part II', D. J. Law, *Harpsichord and fortepiano*, xiii/2 (Spring 2009), pp.24-27

'Modifying Modern Harpsichord Dampers', Paul Y. Irvin, *Harpsichord and fortepiano*, xiv/2 (Spring 2010), p.30-34

'Tailoring the Sound of your Keyboard Instrument, Part 1', Paul Y. Irvin, *Harpsichord and fortepiano*, xvi/1 (Autumn 2011), pp.27-32

'Optimising Harpsichord Staggering', Claudio Di Veroli, *Harpsichord and fortepiano*, xvi/2 (Spring 2012), pp.8-13

'Tailoring the Sound of your Keyboard Instrument, Part II', Paul Y. Irvin, *Harpsichord and fortepiano*, xvi/2 (Spring 2012), pp.20-26

'To Quill or Not to Quill? [M. R. Levoi and R. P. Williams, Denzil Wraight, Tilman Skowroneck]', *Harpsichord and fortepiano*, xvii/1 (Autumn 2012), pp.22-26

'Tailoring the Sound of your Keyboard Instrument Part IV: Musical Pins', Paul Y. Irvin, *Harpsichord and fortepiano*, xviii/1 (Autumn 2013), pp.17-23

'A Practical Guide to Quilling', John Phillips, *Harpsichord and fortepiano*, xviii/1 (Autumn 2013), pp.24-31

'Early keyboard technology instruction in the US', Allan Winkler, *Harpsichord & fortepiano*, xxvi/1 (Autumn 2021), pp.21-32

'Modern vs historical harpsichord plucking', Paul Y. Irvin, *Harpsichord & fortepiano*, xxviii/1 (Autumn 2023), pp.19-21

3.4 Actions and Mechanism

'Quick Jacks for Amateurs', P. Deen, *The English Harpsichord Magazine*, i/3 (October 1974), pp.84-86

'The Wearing Properties of Harpsichord Plectra', *The English Harpsichord Magazine*, i/6 (April 1976), M. R. Levoi and R. P. Williams, pp.172-174

'The Musical Mechanisms of Arnaut de Zwolle', John Lester, *The English Harpsichord Magazine*, iii/3 (October 1982), pp.35-41

'Fortepiano kapsels old and new', Martha Goodway, *Harpsichord and fortepiano*, vi/1 (May 1997), pp.13-16

4. REPERTOIRE

4.1 General

'For Two to Play', Maria Boxall, *The English Harpsichord Magazine*, ii/1 (October 1977), pp.26-27

'New Light on the Early Italian Keyboard Tradition' Maria Boxall, *The English Harpsichord Magazine*, ii/3 (October 1978), pp.71-72

'Paul Hofhaimer', *The English Harpsichord Magazine*, ii/3 (October 1978), pp.72-73

'An Introduction to Restoration Keyboard Music', Terrence Charlston, *Harpsichord and fortepiano*, x/2 (Spring 2006), pp.26-36

'An Introduction to Restoration Keyboard Music II: Bryne, Roberts and Moss', Terrence Charlston, *Harpsichord and fortepiano*, xi/1 (Autumn 2006), pp.14-27

'Women of Note', Diana Ambache, *Harpsichord and fortepiano*, xvi/1 (Autumn 2011), pp.8-11

'The Oriental Miscellany and the Hindustani Air: "Wild but Pleasing when Understood"', Jane Chapman, *Harpsichord and fortepiano*, xvii/2 (Spring 2013), pp.24-30

'Recording the Fitzwilliam Virginal Book', Pieter-Jan Belder, *Harpsichord & fortepiano*, xxiv/2 (Spring 2020), pp.20-23

'Portuguese keyboard music from the second half of the 18th century', Mafalda Nejmeddine, *Harpsichord & fortepiano*, xxvi/1 (Autumn 2021), pp.4-8

'1741: three masterworks of diversity', Claudio Di Veroli, *Harpsichord & fortepiano*, xxvi/2 (Spring 2022), pp.21-26

4.2 J. S. Bach

'Was Bach a Mathematician?', Herbert Anton Kellner, *The English Harpsichord Magazine*, ii/2 (April 1978), pp.32-36

'Bach and the German Clavier', D. E. Dodge, *The English Harpsichord Magazine*, ii/3 (October 1978), pp.67-71

'The Identity of Bach's Clavier', D. E. Dodge, *The English Harpsichord Magazine*, ii/5 (October 1979), pp.116-119

'Das Wohltemperierte Clavier: Tuning & Musical Structure', Herbert Anton Kellner, *The English Harpsichord Magazine*, ii/6 (April 1980), pp.137-140

'The Mathematical Architecture of Bach's Goldberg Variations', Herbert Anton Kellner, *The English Harpsichord Magazine*, ii/8 (April 1981), pp.183-189

'The temperament for Bach's "48"', Michael Thomas, *The English Harpsichord Magazine*, iv/2 (1986), pp.18-21

'How Bach quantified his well-tempered tuning within the FOUR DUETS', Herbert Anton Kellner, *The English Harpsichord Magazine*, iv/2 (1986), pp.21-27

'Back to Bach: *Das Wohltemperirte Clavier* revisited', Stephen Daw, *Harpsichord and fortepiano*, v/2 (April 1995), pp.11-15

'The Brandenburg Concertos: A New Interpretation', Philip Pickett, *Harpsichord and fortepiano*, vi/2 (November 1997), pp.22-32

'Bach Transcribed: A Study in Two Parts', Pamela Nash, *Harpsichord and fortepiano*, vii/1 (Winter 1998), pp.39-43

'Bach Transcribed: Part Two', Pamela Nash, *Harpsichord and fortepiano*, viii/1 (Autumn 1999), pp.23-26

'Bach Transcribed: Part Three', Pamela Nash, *Harpsichord and fortepiano*, viii/2 (Spring 2000), pp.19-23

'Some thoughts on Playing the Goldberg Variations, BWV 988', Richard Leigh Harris, *Harpsichord and fortepiano*, xiv/2 (Spring 2010), pp.16-19

'Unanswered questions: Bach, Forkel, *schellen*, and keyboard touch', Richard Troeger, *Harpsichord and fortepiano*, xxi/1 (Autumn 2016), pp.22-32

'A measured approach to J.S. Bach's Stylus Phantasticus', Claudio Di Veroli, *Harpsichord and fortepiano*, xxi/2 (Spring 2017), pp.17-26

'Learning 'The 48'', Francis Knights, *Harpsichord and fortepiano*, xxiii/1 (Autumn 2018), pp.21-31

'"Because they could never have equaled their father in his style": creativity at the keyboard in the Bach family', David Schulenberg, *Harpsichord & fortepiano*, xxiv/1 (Autumn 2019), pp.4-7

'The musician's bookshelf: J. S. Bach', Francis Knights, *Harpsichord & fortepiano*, xxiv/2 (Spring 2020), p.32

'Bach on the harpsichord – some personal reflections'. Colin Booth, *Harpsichord & fortepiano*, xxv/1 (Autumn 2020), pp.4-10

'Harpsichords in Bach's Germany: an overview', Leonard Schick, *Harpsichord & # fortepiano*, xxvi/2 (Spring 2022), pp.10-20

'1741: three masterworks of diversity', Claudio Di Veroli, *Harpsichord & fortepiano*, xxvi/2 (Spring 2022), pp.21-26

'The *Orgelbüchlein* as pedal clavichord music', Terence Charlston, *Harpsichord & fortepiano*, xxvii/1 (Autumn 2022), pp.11-15

'Forkel's Bach revisited', Claudio Di Veroli, *Harpsichord & fortepiano*, xxvii/2 (Spring 2023), pp.12-19

'Bach at the keyboard: The organist at home', Colin Booth, *Harpsichord & fortepiano*, xxviii/1 (Autumn 2023), pp.8-14

4.3 Couperin family

'Chambonnières versus Louis Couperin: attributing the F major Chaconne', Francis Knights, Pablo Padilla and Dan Tidhar, *Harpsichord and fortepiano*, xxii/1 (Autumn 2017), pp.28-32

'Did Couperin ever play a trill before the beat?', Claudio Di Veroli, *Harpsichord and fortepiano*, vi/1 (May 1997), pp.20-22

'The Architecture of the Ordres [Couperin]', Jane Clark, *Harpsichord and fortepiano*, x/2 (Spring 2006), pp.21-25

'Couperin's *Misterieuse* Fourth Harpsichord Book', Pieter Dirksen, *Harpsichord & fortepiano*, xxiv/1 (Autumn 2019), pp.18-23

'Performing François Couperin's *Les Baricades Mistérieuses*', Claudio di Veroli, *Harpsichord & fortepiano*, xxiv/2 (Spring 2020), pp.15-19

4.4 Scarlatti

'The Performer's Approach to Scarlatti', Richard Lester, *The English Harpsichord Magazine*, i/8 (April 1977), pp.223-226

'Thoughts on Scarlatti's Essercizi per Gravicembalo', Richard Lester, *The English Harpsichord Magazine*, ii/1 (October 1977), pp.10-12, 17-18

'Viscount Fitzwilliam and the English "Scarlatti Sect"', Gerald Gifford, *The Harpsichord and Fortepiano Magazine*, iv/5 (April 1988), pp.113-116

'Flamenco Sketches: Part 1 [Scarlatti]', Richard Lester, *Harpsichord and fortepiano*, xi/1 (Autumn 2006), pp.28-33

'Flamenco Sketches: Part 2 [Scarlatti]', Richard Lester, *Harpsichord and fortepiano*, xi/2 (Spring 2007), pp.12-16

'Scarlatti Sonatas, Step by Step', Penelope Cave, *Harpsichord and fortepiano*, xii/2 (Spring 2008), pp.27-29

'Flamenco sketches (revisited) [Scarlatti]', Richard Lester, *Harpsichord & fortepiano*, xxvi/1 (Autumn 2021), pp.9-15

4.5 Other Composers, A-Z

'William Babell's recently discovered toccatas', Andrew Woolley, *Harpsichord & fortepiano*, xxvi/2 (Spring 2022), pp.27-30

'Why is the "Great *In Nomine*" great? [Bull]', Micaela Schmitz, *Harpsichord and fortepiano*, x/2 (Spring 2006), pp.45-51

'The keyboard music of Charles Burney', Francis Knights, *Harpsichord & fortepiano*, xxv/2 (Spring 2021), pp.13-23

'Buxtehude's Works for Stringed Keyboard Instruments', John Collins, *Harpsichord and fortepiano*, xi/2 (Spring 2007), pp.31-40

'Rediscovering Clementi's *Gradus ad Parnassum*: A New perspective from the Early English Piano', John Khouri, *Harpsichord and fortepiano*, xvii/1 (Autumn 2012), pp.11-14

'Muzio Clementi's contribution to the history of music', Marina Rodríguez Brià, *Harpsichord & fortepiano*, xxv/2 (Spring 2021), pp.24-27

'Girolamo Diruta's "Il Transilvano" and the Early Italian Keyboard Tradition', *The English Harpsichord Magazine*, i/6 (April 1976), Maria Boxall, pp.168-172

'Fingers Crossed: Girolamo Diruta's *Il Transilvano* (1593): A Re-evaluation;, Richard Lester, *Harpsichord and fortepiano*, xvix/2 (Spring 2015), pp.15-26

'Dussek, Broadwood and the Additional Keys', Mora Carroll, *Harpsichord and fortepiano*, viii/1 (Autumn 1999), pp.3-10

'Jan Ladislav Dussek and his music for the extended keyboard compass', Mora Carroll, *Harpsichord and fortepiano*, ix/2 (Summer 2001), pp.8-15

'The Keyboard Music of Hugh Facy', Desmond Hunter, *The Harpsichord and Fortepiano Magazine*, iv/7 (April 1989), pp.173-177

'John Field (1782-1837) and his Piano Music', Gwilym Beechey, *Harpsichord and fortepiano*, viii/2 (Spring 2000), pp.24-27

'Frescobaldi Unmasked: Unravelling Complexities of Interpretation within the Toccatas', Richard Lester, *Harpsichord and fortepiano*, xiii/2 (Spring 2009), pp.10-19

'"Ziegler Variations": On the Goldberg Polonaises: In Search of the Author', Maxim Serebrennikov, *Harpsichord and fortepiano*, xiv/2 (Spring 2010), pp.9-15

'Elisabeth-Claude Jacquet De La Guerre', Pamela Hickman, *Harpsichord and fortepiano*, xvi/1 (Autumn 2011), pp.12-14

'Handel's eight great suites for harpsichord', Gwilym Beechey, *Harpsichord and fortepiano*, vi/1 (May 1997), pp.24-26

'Keyboard Instruments in Haydn's Vienna', Richard Maunder, *Harpsichord and fortepiano*, vii/1 (June 1998), pp.5-10

'Mattheson's Harmony's Monument: the Twelve Suites of 1714: Clues to the Execution of Rhythm in German Baroque Suites', Colin Booth, *Harpsichord and fortepiano*, xv/1 (Autumn 2010), pp.25-30

'Claudio Merulo: Two biographical notes', Glen Wilson, *Harpsichord & fortepiano*, xxvii/1 (Autumn 2022), pp.4-10

'Thomas Morley's Keyboard Music', Gwilyn Beechey, *Harpsichord and fortepiano*, x/1 (Autumn 2002), pp.12-15

'Thomas Morley's Keyboard Music', Gwilym Beechey, *Harpsichord and fortepiano*, xiii/2 (Spring 2009), pp.20-23

'Playing Mozart On The Fortepiano', Christopher Kite, *The Harpsichord and Fortepiano Magazine*, iv/3 (April 1987), pp.52-55

'Mozart and the Clavier', Neil Coleman, *Harpsichord and fortepiano*, xi/2 (Spring 2007), pp.20-30

'Mozart and the Clavier – a Supplement', Neil Coleman, *Harpsichord and fortepiano*, xii/1 (Autumn 2007), pp.30-34

'An Overview of the Keyboard Music of Bernardo Pasquini (1637-1710)', John Collins, *Harpsichord and fortepiano*, xv/1 (Autumn 2010), pp.17-24

'Inégalité and Rameau's Concerts: a case of "Ille dixit"?', Claudio Di Veroli, *Harpsichord and fortepiano*, viii/2 (Spring 2000), pp.28-34

'Rudolf Straube', Kah-Ming Ng, *Harpsichord and fortepiano*, xv/2 (Spring 2011), pp.27-28

'"Eloquent Fingers": indications and implications of fingering in Sweelinck's keyboard music', Kathryn Cok, *Harpsichord & fortepiano*, xxvi/2 (Spring 2022), pp.4-9

'Telemann's Harpsichord Music', Edgar Hunt, *The English Harpsichord Magazine*, iii/1 (October 1981), p.16

'"An Eagle over Falcons": recording harpsichord music by John Worgan (1724-1790)', Julian Perkins, *Harpsichord & fortepiano*, xxvi/1 (Autumn 2021), pp.29-30

4.5 Contemporary Music

'The Challenge of New Music', Jane Chapman, *Harpsichord and fortepiano*, v/1 (October 1994), pp.7-13

'*Philibuster*: New music for the fortepiano', Marc Reichow and Richard Sims, *Harpsichord and fortepiano*, v/3 (October 1995), pp.23-29

'Dance to the Music of Time [Delius, *Dance for Harpsichord*]', Penelope Cave, *Harpsichord and fortepiano*, vi/1 (May 1997), pp.7-9

'The Naked Truth: Composing for the Harpsichord', Kevin Malone, *Harpsichord and fortepiano*, vii/1 (Winter 1998), pp.5-9

'New Music Focus', Penelope Cave, Bridget Cunningham, Elaine Comparone, Pamela Nash, *Harpsichord and fortepiano*, xii/1 (Autumn 2007), pp.22-29

'Composing *Toccata de Roça* for Solo Harpsichord', Calimerio Soares, *Harpsichord and fortepiano*, xii/2 (Spring 2008), pp.15-26

'The Once and Future Harpsichord: The Aliénor Competition for Composition', Barbara Norton, *Harpsichord and fortepiano*, xiii/1 (Autumn 2008), pp.6-7

'Everything New is Old Again – Part I', Grant Colburn with Micaela Schmitz, *Harpsichord and fortepiano*, xiv/1 (Autumn 2009), pp.18-23

'Everything New is Old Again – Part II', Grant Colburn, Fernando De Luca, Micaela Schmitz, *Harpsichord and fortepiano*, xiv/2 (Spring 2010), pp.20-29

5. PERFORMANCE and TEACHING

5.1 Performance Practice

'The "Incy Wincy Spider"', Maria Boxall, *The English Harpsichord Magazine*, i/4 (April 1975), pp.106-108 [see also i/5, pp.154-155]

'The Position of Grace Signs in MS. Sources of English Virginal Music', Desmond Hunter, *The English Harpsichord Magazine*, iii/5 (October 1983), pp.82-91

'Aspects of Thorough Bass', David Roblou, *The Harpsichord and Fortepiano Magazine*, iv/5 (April 1988), pp.106-112

'Inégalité and Rameau's Concerts: a case of "Ille dixit"?', Claudio Di Veroli, *Harpsichord and fortepiano*, viii/2 (Spring 2000), pp.28-34

'Renaissance Harpsichord Renaissance: Philip Pickett's approach to performance practice and why he commissioned the Trasuntino copy', Alison Holloway, *Harpsichord and fortepiano*, ix/1 (Spring 2001), pp.3-6

Mattheson's Harmony's Monument: the Twelve Suites of 1714: Clues to the Execution of Rhythm in German Baroque Suites', Colin Booth, *Harpsichord and fortepiano*, xv/1 (Autumn 2010), pp.25-30 [and see correction in *HF*, xv/2 (Spring 2011), p.3]

'"Texture and Playing Style in Classic Keyboard Music', Richard Troeger, *Harpsichord and fortepiano*, xvi/2 (Spring 2012), pp.27-32

'Fingers Crossed: Girolamo Diruta's *Il Transilvano* (1593): A Re-evaluation;', Richard Lester, *Harpsichord and fortepiano*, xvix/2 (Spring 2015), pp.15-26

'Trills and frills, a variety of inventions: the North Italian art of Diminutione and Tremoli', Richard Lester, *Harpsichord and fortepiano*, xx/1 (Autumn 2015), pp.11-26

'Registration matters: analyzing Italian Renaissance registration', Richard Lester, *Harpsichord and fortepiano*, xxi/1 (Autumn 2016), pp.15-21

'Unanswered questions: Bach, Forkel, *schellen*, and keyboard touch', Richard Troeger, *Harpsichord and fortepiano*, xxi/1 (Autumn 2016), pp.22-32

'Fortepiano-harpsichord duos in two eighteenth-century salons', Rebecca Cypess, *Harpsichord and fortepiano*, xxii/2 (Spring 2018), pp.20-25

'Controlling dynamics on the harpsichord: some examples of techniques employed by 18th-century composers', Colin Booth, *Harpsichord & fortepiano*, xxvi/1 (Autumn 2021), pp.16-20

'Music and criticism: Revisiting George Malcolm's thoughts on authenticity', Richard Lester, *Harpsichord & fortepiano*, xxviii/1 (Autumn 2023), pp.28-30

5.2 Fingering and Technique

'The "Incy Wincy Spider"', Maria Boxall, *The English Harpsichord Magazine*, i/4 (April 1975), pp.106-108 [see also i/5, pp.154-155]

'Elementary Harpsichord Technique', Roy Truby, *The English Harpsichord Magazine*, i/5 (October 1975), pp.132-134

'Girolamo Diruta's "Il Transilvano" and the Early Italian Keyboard Tradition', *The English Harpsichord Magazine*, i/6 (April 1976), Maria Boxall, pp.168-172

'"My Lady Nevell's Book" and Old Fingerings', Ton Koopman, *The English Harpsichord Magazine*, ii/1 (October 1977), pp.5-10

'Further Light on Early Keyboard Fingerings', Desmond Hunter, *The (English) Harpsichord Magazine*, iv/1 (October 1985), pp.2-7

'Early Keyboard Fingerings: A select Bibliography', Mark Lindley, *The (English) Harpsichord Magazine*, iii/8 (April 1985), pp.155-161 [see also EHM iv/1 (October 1985), p.15]

'Revisiting keyboard technique', Micaela Schmitz, *Harpsichord and fortepiano*, xxi/2 (Spring 2017), pp.28-31

'Baroque Keyboard Fingering and Present-Day Practice', Claudio Di Veroli, *Harpsichord and fortepiano*, xxiii/2 (Spring 2019), pp.27-34

5.3 Ornamentation

'The Position of Grace Signs in MS. Sources of English Virginal Music', Desmond Hunter, *The English Harpsichord Magazine*, iii/5 (October 1983), pp.82-91

'Did Couperin ever play a trill before the beat?', Claudio Di Veroli, *Harpsichord and fortepiano*, vi/1 (May 1997), pp.20-22

'The Authority of the Bevin table in the interpretation of ornament sign in Elizabethan virginal music', Asako Hirabayashi, *Harpsichord and fortepiano*, ix/1 (Spring 2001), pp.24-30

'Trills and frills, a variety of inventions: the North Italian art of Diminutione and Tremoli', Richard Lester, *Harpsichord and fortepiano*, xx/1 (Autumn 2015), pp.11-26

5.4 Basso Continuo

'Aspects of Thorough Bass', David Roblou, *The Harpsichord and Fortepiano Magazine*, iv/5 (April 1988), pp.106-112

'Behind the Mask: Continuo in Monteverdi's *L'Orfeo*', Philip Pickett, *Harpsichord and fortepiano*, vii/1 (Winter 1998), pp.10-16

'"…dovendosi sonare piu piano, che sij possibile…": style in Italian harpsichord basso continuo realization', Giulia Nuti, *Harpsichord and fortepiano*, vii/1 (Winter 1998), pp.18-26

'Techniques of Baroque Accompaniment', Robert Webb, *Harpsichord and fortepiano*, vii/1 (Winter 1998), pp.28-34

'Book for Thoroughbass (1786) owned by Ms. Avdot'ja Ivanova: Pages from one lady's music album during the period of Catherine the Great', Maxim Serebrennikov, *Harpsichord and fortepiano*, xvi/1 (Autumn 2011), pp.21-26

5.5 Sources and Editions

'The Broadwood Books: I', Charles Mould, *The Harpsichord Magazine*, i/1 (October 1973), pp.19-23

'The Broadwood Books; II', Charles Mould, *The English Harpsichord Magazine*, i/2 (April 1974), pp.47-53

'"My Lady Nevell's Book" and Old Fingerings', Ton Koopman, *The English Harpsichord Magazine*, ii/1 (October 1977), pp.5-10

'The Harpsichord Master of 1697 and its relationship to contemporary instruction & playing', Maria Boxall, *The English Harpsichord Magazine*, ii/8 (April 1981), pp.178-183

'The Harpsichord Master of 1697', Maria Boxall, *The English Harpsichord Magazine*, ii/8 (April 1981), pp.178-183

'Ammerbach's 1583 Exercises', Mark Lindley, *The English Harpsichord Magazine*, iii/4 (April 1983), pp.58-66

'Is there an Enigma in Werckmeister's "Musicalische Temperatur"?', Herbert Anton Kellner, *The (English) Harpsichord Magazine*, iii/7 (October 1984), pp.134-136

'One typographical Enigma in Werckmeister, "Musicalische Temperatur"', Herbert Anton Kellner, *The (English) Harpsichord Magazine*, iii/8 (April 1985), pp.146-151

'Did Werckmeister already know the tuning of J. S. Bach for the "48"?', Herbert Anton Kellner, *The (English) Harpsichord Magazine*, iv/1 (October 1985), pp.7-11

'Do we know how to read Urtext editions? *or* the case of the Missing Dot', Malcolm Bilson, *Harpsichord and fortepiano*, v/2 (April 1995), pp.23-30

'Christoph Benjamin Schmidtchen and his Small Keyboard Tutor', Gwilym Beechey, *Harpsichord and fortepiano*, vii/1 (June 1998), pp.29-34

'Some rare sources of Georgian harpsichord music in the Library of Arnold Dolmetsch (1858-1940)', Gerald Gifford, *Harpsichord and fortepiano*, ix/2 (Summer 2001), pp.20-25

'Eighteenth Century English Publications of Keyboard Music in the Library of Burghley House, Stamford', Gerald Gifford, *Harpsichord and fortepiano*, x/1 (Autumn 2002), pp.16-21

'A Quest for Music: Treasures from the University of Leiden Library Revealed, with a Special Focus on Dutch Music 1650-1750', Kathryn Cok, *Harpsichord and fortepiano*, x/2 (Spring 2006), pp.37

'The venerable "Boalch" - ready for its next 70 years', John Watson, *Harpsichord & fortepiano*, xxviii/1 (Autumn 2023), pp.39-41

'Full Circle? Observations on keyboard music to c.1630 in Musica Britannica and some thoughts about the future', David J. Smith, *Harpsichord & fortepiano*, xxviii/1 (Autumn 2023), pp.42-44

5.6 Teaching

'The Harpsichord Master of 1697 and its relationship to contemporary instruction & playing', Maria Boxall, *The English Harpsichord Magazine*, ii/8 (April 1981), pp.178-183

'The Harpsichord Master of 1697', Maria Boxall, *The English Harpsichord Magazine*, ii/8 (April 1981), pp.178-183

'Ammerbach's 1583 Exercises', Mark Lindley, *The English Harpsichord Magazine*, iii/4 (April 1983), pp.58-66

'Christoph Benjamin Schmidtchen and his Small Keyboard Tutor', Gwilym Beechey, *Harpsichord and fortepiano*, vii/1 (June 1998), pp.29-34

'Practice Matters: Preparing the performing score to ease communication between the notes, the brain and the fingers', Penelope Cave, *Harpsichord and fortepiano*, ix/2 (Summer 2001), pp.16-19

'Learning 'The 48', Francis Knights, *Harpsichord and fortepiano*, xxiii/1 (Autumn 2018), pp.21-31

'A perspective on historical keyboard playing in the UK', Terence Charlston, *Harpsichord & fortepiano*, xxviii/1 (Autumn 2023), pp.26-27

'Clavichord gatherings', Richard Troeger, *Harpsichord & fortepiano*, xxviii/1 (Autumn # 2023), pp.31-34

'Swimming upstream: Reflections of an American harpsichordist from across "The Pond"', Mark Kroll, *Harpsichord & fortepiano*, xxviii/1 (Autumn 2023), pp.35-38

6. COLLECTIONS & ORGANIZATIONS

'The Instrumental Museum – Lisbon', L. A. Esteves Pereria, *The English Harpsichord Magazine*, i/7 (October 1976), pp.197-198

'The John Loosemore Centre for Organ and Early Music', Jonathan Garland, *The English Harpsichord Magazine*, ii/6 (April 1980), pp.134-136

'Collections – Finchcocks', Warwick Henry Cole, *The Harpsichord and Fortepiano Magazine*, iv/3 (April 1987), pp.63-65

'St. Cecilia's Hall And The Russell Collection', John Raymond, *The Harpsichord and Fortepiano Magazine*, iv/4 (October 1987), pp.86-91

'The Metropolitan Museum of Art', Laurence Libin, *The Harpsichord and Fortepiano Magazine*, iv/7 (April 1989), pp.178-184

'A Collection in distress? The Colt Clavier Collection at 50', *Harpsichord and fortepiano*, v/1 (October 1994), pp.30-32

'Underground Movement [Harley Foundation]', Alison Holloway, *Harpsichord and fortepiano*, vii/1 (June 1998), pp.35-38

'*pian'e fortino*: The Neumeyer Collection and its curator', Alison Holloway, *Harpsichord and fortepiano*, vii/1 (Winter 1998), pp.35-38

'The Broadwood Trust: Grand Finale', Katrina Burnett, *Harpsichord and fortepiano*, ix/2 (Summer 2001), pp.3-7

'York Gate Collections: Keyboards', Aaron Shorr, Roy Howat, *Harpsichord and fortepiano*, x/2 (Spring 2006), pp.5-7

'A Glimpse of the Tagliavini Collection of Musical Instruments', María Virginia Rolfo, *Harpsichord and fortepiano*, xvi/1 (Autumn 2011), pp.15-20

'Keyboards in Vermillion: with John Koster', *Harpsichord and fortepiano*, xvi/2 (Spring 2012), pp.14-19

'Keyboard instruments – some collective thoughts', Paul Simmonds, *Harpsichord & fortepiano*, xxvi/1 (Autumn 2021), pp.21-28

7. INTERVIEWS and PROFILES

'Interview with Derek Adlam', Paula Woods, *Harpsichord and fortepiano*, xii/1 (Autumn 2007), pp.14-18

'Isolde Ahlgrimm and Vienna's Historic Keyboard Revival', Peter Watchorn, *Harpsichord and fortepiano*, vi/2 (November 1997), pp.10-17

'Isolde Ahlgrimm: discography, performers, publications and instruments', Peter Watchorn, *Harpsichord and fortepiano*, vii/1 (June 1998), pp.14-22

'Interview with Kristian Bezuidenhout', Pamela Hickman, *Harpsichord and fortepiano*, xxii/1 (Autumn 2017), pp.12-19

'Women in Early Music: Interview with Pamela Nash; Interview with Emer Buckley; Interview with Medea Bindewald', *Harpsichord and fortepiano*, xxiii/2 (Spring 2019), pp.19-26

'Maria Boxall Interviewed', David Lasocki, *The English Harpsichord Magazine*, ii/1 (October 1977), pp.2-4

'An interview with Ronald Brautigam', Alison Holloway, *Harpsichord and fortepiano*, vii/1 (June 1998), pp.11-13

'Women in Early Music: Interview with Pamela Nash; Interview with Emer Buckley; Interview with Medea Bindewald', *Harpsichord and fortepiano*, xxiii/2 (Spring 2019), pp.19-26

'Interview with Carole Cerasi', Pamela Hickman, *Harpsichord & fortepiano*, xxv/2 (Spring 2021), pp.37-40

'A Performance Practice for the 21st Century: interview with Jane Chapman, Part One', Pamela Nash, *Harpsichord and fortepiano*, vi/2 (November 1997), pp.6-10

'A Performance Practice for the 21st Century: interview with Jane Chapman, Part Two', Pamela Nash, *Harpsichord and fortepiano*, vii/1 (June 1998), pp.23-28

'Interview with Terence Charlston', Pamela Hickman, *Harpsichord and fortepiano*, xxi/1 (Autumn 2016), pp.8-14

'Interview Jane Clark Dodgson in her 90th year', Pamela Nash, *Harpsichord and fortepiano*, xxii/2 (Spring 2018), pp.26-31

'An Interview with Maggie Cole', *The Harpsichord and Fortepiano Magazine*, iv/6 (October 1988), pp.146-149

'An interview with Maggie Cole', Pamela Hickman, *Harpsichord and fortepiano*, xx/2 (Spring 2016), pp.16-21

'Interview with Dr. Stephen Coles', Kathryn Cok, *Harpsichord and fortepiano*, x/2 (Spring 2006), pp.12-13

'Inside Restoration: An Interview Of Ben Marks and Lucy Coad', *Harpsichord and fortepiano*, xiii/2 (Spring 2009), pp.6-8

'Interview with Alan Curtis and Bruce Kennedy', Giulia Nuti, *Harpsichord and fortepiano*, xii/1 (Autumn 2007), pp.19-21

'An Interview with Stephen Dodgson', Pamela Nash, *Harpsichord and fortepiano*, x/1 (Autumn 2002), pp.3-11

'Ruth Dyson, an Interview', [Edgar Hunt], *The English Harpsichord Magazine*, i/5 (October 1975), pp.130-132

'Egarr, to please [interview with Richard Egarr]', Alison Holloway, *Harpsichord and fortepiano*, vi/1 (May 1997), pp.10-12

'Interview with Mahan Esfahani', Pamela Hickman, *Harpsichord and fortepiano*, xvix/2 (Spring 2015), pp.27-30

'Kenneth Gilbert: An Interview', Edgar Hunt, *The English Harpsichord Magazine*, i/3 (October 1974), pp.66-69

'Interview: Christoph Hammer', Pamela Hickman, *Harpsichord & fortepiano*, xxiv/2 (Spring 2020), pp.28-31

'Interview with Bexley Workshops: Maintenance and Tuning Courses [Andrew Wooderson, Edmund Handy]', pp.10-11

'Interview of Myrna Herzog, New Square Piano Owner', Pamela Hickman [with David Shemer], *Harpsichord and fortepiano*, xv/1 (Autumn 2010), pp.4-5

'Interview with Douglas Hollick', Graham Sadler, *Harpsichord and fortepiano*, xviii/2 (Spring 2014), pp.18-21

'Frank Hubbard Interviewed', Tom McGeary, *The English Harpsichord Magazine*, i/4 (April 1975), pp.98-105

'Interview with Paul Irvin', Richard Troeger, *Harpsichord and fortepiano*, xx/2 (Spring 2016), pp.9-15

'Interview with Michael Johnson', Paula Woods, *Harpsichord and fortepiano*, xviii/1 (Autumn 2013), pp.13-16

'An interview with Sharona Joshua', Alison Holloway, *Harpsichord and fortepiano*, vi/2 (November 1997), pp.18-19

'Interview with Alan Curtis and Bruce Kennedy', Giulia Nuti, *Harpsichord and fortepiano*, xii/1 (Autumn 2007), pp.19-21

'Interview with Andreas Kilström', Hila Katz, *Harpsichord & fortepiano*, xxvii/1 (Autumn 2022), pp.25-28

'Igor Kipnis: A Meeting', [Edgar Hunt], *The English Harpsichord Magazine*, i/6 (April 1976), pp.166-167

'Igor Kipnis talks to Elaine Hoffman Baruch', *Harpsichord and fortepiano*, viii/1 (Autumn 1999), pp.11-22

'A Brief Chat with Henk Klop', Micaela Schmitz, *Harpsichord and fortepiano*, xviii/1 (Autumn 2013), p.11

'Ton Koopman: A Meeting', [Edgar Hunt], *The English Harpsichord Magazine*, i/8 (April 1977), p.222

'Interview with Ton Koopman', Kathryn Cok, *Harpsichord and fortepiano*, xi/1 (Autumn 2006), pp.11-13

'Keyboards in Vermillion: with John Koster', *Harpsichord and fortepiano*, xvi/2 (Spring 2012), pp.14-19

'Interview: Maintaining Original Instruments and Allowing Access', Andrew Lamb, *Harpsichord and fortepiano*, xv/2 (Spring 2011), pp.12-15

'David Law: Harpsichord Maker', *The English Harpsichord Magazine*, iii/3 (October 1982), pp.41-43

'Gustav Leonhardt: An Interview', Edgar Hunt, *The English Harpsichord Magazine*, i/2 (April 1974), pp.34-35, 63

'Interview with Richard Lester', Paula Woods, *Harpsichord & fortepiano*, xxvi/2 (Spring 2022), pp.35-38

'Interview with Robert Levin', Pamela Nash, *Harpsichord and fortepiano*, xxiii/2 (Spring 2019), pp.10-12

'George Malcolm, C.B.E.: An Interview', Edgar Hunt, *The Harpsichord Magazine*, i/1 (October 1973), pp.2-5

'Inside Restoration: An Interview of Ben Marks and Lucy Coad', *Harpsichord and fortepiano*, xiii/2 (Spring 2009), pp.6-8

'Interview: Orhan Memed', Francis Knights, *Harpsichord & fortepiano*, xxiv/1 (Autumn 2019), pp.24-26

'Interview with Marina Minkin', Pamela Hickman, *Harpsichord and fortepiano*, xviii/1 (Autumn 2013), pp.8-10

'Interview with harpsichord maker Milan Misina', Pamela Nash, *Harpsichord & fortepiano*, xxviii/1 (Autumn 2023), pp.45-47

'Interview: Gideon Meir', Pamela Hickman, *Harpsichord and fortepiano*, xv/2 (Spring 2011), pp.29-33

'A Question of Cultural Identity', Motoko Nabeshima, *Harpsichord and fortepiano*, v/3 (October 1995), pp.7-10

'Women in Early Music: Interview with Pamela Nash; Interview with Emer Buckley; Interview with Medea Bindewald', *Harpsichord and fortepiano*, xxiii/2 (Spring 2019), pp.19-26

'"A music of surprise and delight": An interview with James Nicolson', Dave Gayman, *Harpsichord and fortepiano*, v/3 (October 1995), pp.20-23

'Trevor Pinnock Interviewed', *The Harpsichord and Fortepiano Magazine*, iv/7 (April 1989), pp.168-172

'A Visit to John Rawson', *The English Harpsichord Magazine*, iii/6 (April 1984), pp.112-115

'Peter Redstone: Harpsichord Maker', [Edgar Hunt], *The English Harpsichord Magazine*, ii/7 (October 1980), pp.163-164

'Interpretation with respect: An interview with Christophe Rousset', David Bray, *Harpsichord and fortepiano*, v/1 (October 1994), pp.19-21

'Interview with Tilman Skowroneck', Pamela Hickman, *Harpsichord and fortepiano*, xvii/2 (Spring 2013), pp.5-11

'Interview with Michael Tsalka', Pamela Hickman, *Harpsichord and fortepiano*, xxi/2 (Spring 2017), pp.9-16

'"Catching the rhythm": An interview with Andreas Staier', David Bray, *Harpsichord and fortepiano*, v/2 (April 1995), pp.17-19

'An Interview With Melvyn Tan', Warwick Henry Cole, *The Harpsichord and Fortepiano Magazine*, iv/4 (October 1987), pp.74-78

'Interview with Richard Taylor', Paula Woods, *Harpsichord & fortepiano*, xxv/1 (Autumn 2020), pp.28-30

'Interview with Richard Troeger', *Harpsichord and fortepiano*, xviii/2 (Spring 2014), pp.10-17

'An interview with Olga Tverskaya', Alison Holloway, *Harpsichord and fortepiano*, vi/2 (November 1997), pp.33-34

'Luis Gonzalez Uriol Interviewed', Susanne Shapiro, *The English Harpsichord Magazine*, ii/4 (April 1979), pp.82-83

'Interview with Jory Vinikour', Pamela Hickman, *Harpsichord and fortepiano*, xxii/2 (Spring 2018), pp.12-19

'An American in Paris [interview with Kenneth Weiss]', Alison Holloway, *Harpsichord and fortepiano*, vi/1 (May 1997), pp.17-19

'Interview with Bexley Workshops: Maintenance and Tuning Courses [Andrew Wooderson, Edmund Handy]', pp.10-11

8. OBITUARIES

Don Angle, *Harpsichord and fortepiano*, xv/2 (Spring 2011), p.4

Valda Aveling, *Harpsichord and fortepiano*, xii/2 (Spring 2008), pp.5-6

Joan Benson, *Harpsichord & fortepiano*, xxv/1 (Autumn 2020), pp.21-27

David Bolton, *Harpsichord and fortepiano*, xii/2 (Spring 2008), pp.4-5

Frans Brüggen, *Harpsichord and fortepiano*, xix/1 (Autumn 2014), pp.125-29

John Challis, *The English Harpsichord Magazine*, i/5 (October 1975), p.155

Elisabeth Chojnacka, *Harpsichord and fortepiano*, xxii/1 (Autumn 2017), p.4

Martha Novak Clinkscale, *Harpsichord and fortepiano*, xv/2 (Spring 2011), p.4

Peter Collins, *Harpsichord and fortepiano*, xx/2 (Spring 2016), pp.4-5

Elizabeth de la Porte, *Harpsichord & fortepiano*, xxv/2 (Spring 2021), pp.35-36

Huguette Dreyfus, *Harpsichord and fortepiano*, xxi/2 (Spring 2017), p.5

Ruth Dyson, *Harpsichord and fortepiano*, vi/2 (November 1997), p.36

David Evans, *Harpsichord and fortepiano*, xxiii/2 (Spring 2019), pp.13-18

Kenneth Gilbert, *Harpsichord & fortepiano*, xxv/2 (Spring 2021), pp.32-34

Elizabeth Goble, *The English Harpsichord Magazine*, iii/2 (April 1982), p.32

Thomas Goff, *The English Harpsichord Magazine*, i/5 (October 1975), p.155

Ronald Haas, *Harpsichord and fortepiano*, xx/1 (Autumn 2015), p.7

Christopher Hogwood, *Harpsichord and fortepiano*, xvix/2 (Spring 2015), pp.10-13

Frank Hubbard, *The English Harpsichord Magazine*, i/6 (April 1976), p.185
Philip James, *The English Harpsichord Magazine*, i/3 (October 1974), p.92
Geraint Jones, *Harpsichord and fortepiano*, vii/1 (Winter 1998), p.60
Brian Jordan, *Harpsichord and fortepiano*, xv/2 (Spring 2011), p.4
Owen H. Jorgensen, *Harpsichord and fortepiano*, xiv/2 (Spring 2010), p.5
Christopher Kite, *Harpsichord and fortepiano*, v/1 (October 1994), p.7
Gustav Leonhardt, *Harpsichord and fortepiano*, xvii/1 (Autumn 2012), pp.15-21
Thornton Lofthouse, *The English Harpsichord Magazine*, i/3 (October 1974), pp.91-92
Kenneth Mobbs, *Harpsichord and fortepiano*, xxii/2 (Spring 2018), pp.7-9
Mary Jeanette Mobbs, *Harpsichord and fortepiano*, xvii/1 (Autumn 2012), pp.5-6
Gordon Murray, *Harpsichord and fortepiano*, xxi/2 (Spring 2017), pp.5-6
Hans Neupert, *The English Harpsichord Magazine*, ii/8 (April 1981), p.200
Joseph Payne, *Harpsichord and fortepiano*, xii/2 (Spring 2008), p.4
Mary Potts, *The English Harpsichord Magazine*, iii/4 (April 1983), p.79
J. J. K. Rhodes, *The English Harpsichord Magazine*, iv/2 (1986), p.32
Edwin M. Ripin, *The English Harpsichord Magazine*, i/6 (April 1976), p.185
Malcolm Rose, *Harpsichord & fortepiano*, xxvii/2 (Spring 2023), pp.34-35
Zuzana Ružicková, *Harpsichord and fortepiano*, xxii/1 (Autumn 2017), pp.4-5
Heather Slade-Lipkin, *Harpsichord and fortepiano*, xxiii/1 (Autumn 2018), pp.10-15
Martin Skowroneck, *Harpsichord and fortepiano*, xix/1 (Autumn 2014), pp.10-16
David Jacques Way, *Harpsichord and fortepiano*, v/1 (October 1994), p.7
Clifford Charles West, *Harpsichord and fortepiano*, xvi/1 (Autumn 2011), p.3
Peter Whale, *Harpsichord and fortepiano*, v/1 (October 1994), p.7
Dennis Woolley, *Harpsichord and fortepiano*, xvii/2 (Spring 2013), p.2
Wolfgang Zuckermann, *Harpsichord and fortepiano*, xxiii/2 (Spring 2019), p.5

9. MISCELLANEOUS

'Notes and Corrections to former Articles and New Information', Michael Thomas, *The English Harpsichord Magazine*, i/7 (October 1976), pp.211-219
'Further Thoughts and Notes', Michael Thomas, *The English Harpsichord Magazine*, i/8 (April 1977), pp.223-235
'Harpsichord Tone Colour', John Paul, *The English Harpsichord Magazine*, ii/1 (October 1977), pp.22-26
'The Nineteenth-Century View of the Old Harpsichord', P. Sween, *The English Harpsichord Magazine*, ii/4 (April 1979), pp.92-95
'L'Orgue et le Clavecin', *The English Harpsichord Magazine*, ii/6 (April 1980), pp.141-143
'A Harpsichord Odyssey (1)', Edgar Hunt, *The English Harpsichord Magazine*, ii/8 (April 1981), pp.190-194
'A Harpsichord Odyssey (II)', Edgar Hunt, *The English Harpsichord Magazine*, iii/1 (October 1981), pp.4-7

'Towards Boalch III', Charles Mould, *The Harpsichord and Fortepiano Magazine*, iv/3 (April 1987), pp.56-59

'Viscount Fitzwilliam and the English "Scarlatti Sect"', Gerald Gifford, *The Harpsichord and Fortepiano Magazine*, iv/5 (April 1988), pp.113-116

'Monteverdi on the road', Simon Neal, *Harpsichord and fortepiano*, v/1 (October 1994), pp.22-25

'Early keyboards in Argentina', Claudio Di Veroli, *Harpsichord and fortepiano*, vi/2 (November 1997), pp.20-21

'Pick up your fingers, prick up your ears', Gary Blaise, *Harpsichord and fortepiano*, viii/2 (Spring 2000), pp.6-18

'Losing their heads?', Andrew Stewart, *Harpsichord and fortepiano*, ix/1 (Spring 2001), pp.14-15

'Keyboard Instruments & Quotation: Using a Quotation from C.P.E. Bach', Penelope Cave, *Harpsichord and fortepiano*, x/2 (Spring 2006), pp.19-20

'The harpsichord in Brazil', Calimerio Soares, *Harpsichord and fortepiano*, xi/2 (Spring 2007), pp.17-19

'An Overview of Pedal Harpsichord Recordings', Mark Ganullin, *Harpsichord and fortepiano*, xi/2 (Spring 2007), pp.41-44

'Le Clavecin en France', Kasia Tomczak-Feltrin, *Harpsichord and fortepiano*, xii/2 (Spring 2008), pp.30-32

'An Approach to Recreating Historical Sound: Part 1', Paul Y. Irvin, *Harpsichord and fortepiano*, xii/2 (Spring 2008), pp.33-38

'An Approach to Recreating Historical Sound: Part II', Paul Y. Irvin, *Harpsichord and fortepiano*, xiii/1 (Autumn 2008), pp.21-27

AUTHOR INDEX

This list of articles is alphabetical by author, then by date of publication. It does not include Reviews: reports, editorials, news, letters or music supplements, for which see the Main Index, p.3.

A

Barry Ainslie, 'Harpsichord Construction in Canada', *The English Harpsichord Magazine*, ii/3 (October 1978), pp.58-62

Diana Ambache, 'Women of Note', *Harpsichord and fortepiano*, xvi/1 (Autumn 2011), pp.8-11

Caperton Andersson with Richard Kingston, 'Makers' Reports: The Birth of a Harpsichord: Richard Kingston's Opus #333', *Harpsichord and fortepiano*, xiv/2 (Spring 2010), pp.4-5

Andrew Appel, 'Remembering Kenneth Gilbert', *Harpsichord & fortepiano*, xxv/2 (Spring 2021), pp.32-34

B

Christopher Barlow, 'The Clavisimbalum of Henri Arnaut de Zwolle c 1440', *Harpsichord and fortepiano*, x/2 (Spring 2006), pp.41-44

-------, 'A Renaissance Piano?', *Harpsichord and fortepiano*, xv/1 (Autumn 2010), pp.15-16

-------, 'The Fluid Piano', *Harpsichord and fortepiano*, xv/2 (Spring 2011), pp.16-18

Peter Bavington, 'An Early Clavycytherium Reconstructed', *The English Harpsichord Magazine*, iii/6 (April 1984), pp.106-111

Gwilym Beechey, 'Handel's eight great suites for harpsichord', *Harpsichord and fortepiano*, vi/1 (May 1997), pp.24-26

-------, 'Christoph Benjamin Schmidtchen and his Small Keyboard Tutor', *Harpsichord and fortepiano*, vii/1 (June 1998), pp.29-34

-------, 'John Field (1782-1837) and his Piano Music', *Harpsichord and fortepiano*, viii/2 (Spring 2000), pp.24-27

-------, 'Thomas Morley's Keyboard Music', *Harpsichord and fortepiano*, x/1 (Autumn 2002), pp.12-15

-------, 'Thomas Morley's Keyboard Music', *Harpsichord and fortepiano*, xiii/2 (Spring 2009), pp.20-23

Pieter-Jan Belder, 'Recording the Fitzwilliam Virginal Book', *Harpsichord & fortepiano*, xxiv/2 (Spring 2020), pp.20-23

John R. Bell, 'Restoring the 'golden' harpsichord', *Harpsichord & fortepiano*, xxviii/1 (Autumn 2023), pp.15-18

Malcolm Bilson, 'Do we know how to read Urtext editions? *or* the case of the Missing Dot', *Harpsichord and fortepiano*, v/2 (April 1995), pp.23-30

Gary Blaise, 'Pick up your fingers, prick up your ears', *Harpsichord and fortepiano*, viii/2 (Spring 2000), pp.6-18

Colin Booth, 'The Pedal Harpsichord – A Recent Reconstruction', *The Harpsichord and Fortepiano Magazine*, iv/5 (April 1988), pp.117-120

-------, 'Mattheson's Harmony's Monument: the Twelve Suites of 1714: Clues to the Execution of Rhythm in German Baroque Suites', *Harpsichord and fortepiano*, xv/1 (Autumn 2010), pp.25-30 [and see correction in *HF*, xv/2 (Spring 2011), p.3]

-------, 'Bach on the harpsichord – some personal reflections', *Harpsichord & fortepiano*, xxv/1 (Autumn 2020), pp.4-10

-------, 'Controlling dynamics on the harpsichord: some examples of techniques employed by 18th-century composers', *Harpsichord & fortepiano*, xxvi/1 (Autumn 2021), pp.16-20

-------, 'Bach at the keyboard: The organist at home', *Harpsichord & fortepiano*, xxviii/1 (Autumn 2023), pp.8-14

Maria Boxall, 'The "Incy Wincy Spider"', *The English Harpsichord Magazine*, i/4 (April 1975), pp.106-108 [see also i/5, pp.154-155]

-------, 'Girolamo Diruta's "Il Transilvano" and the Early Italian Keyboard Tradition', *The English Harpsichord Magazine*, i/6 (April 1976), pp.168-172

-------, 'For Two to Play', *The English Harpsichord Magazine*, ii/1 (October 1977), pp.26-27

-------, 'New Light on the Early Italian Keyboard Tradition', *The English Harpsichord Magazine*, ii/3 (October 1978), pp.71-72

-------, 'The Harpsichord Master of 1697 and its relationship to contemporary instruction & playing', *The English Harpsichord Magazine*, ii/8 (April 1981), pp.178-183

-------, 'The Harpsichord Master of 1697', *The English Harpsichord Magazine*, ii/8 (April 1981), pp.178-183

Marina Rodríguez Brià, 'Muzio Clementi's contribution to the history of music', *Harpsichord & fortepiano*, xxv/2 (Spring 2021), pp.24-27

Peter Brownlee, 'Remembering Joan Benson', *Harpsichord & fortepiano*, xxv/1 (Autumn 2020), pp.21-27

Will Bruggmann, 'A Harpsichord from Switzerland', *The English Harpsichord Magazine*, ii/2 (April 1978), pp.40-44

Katarina Burnett, 'The Broadwood Trust: Grand Finale', *Harpsichord and fortepiano*, ix/2 (Summer 2001), pp.3-7

C

Mora Carroll, 'Dussek, Broadwood and the Additional Keys', *Harpsichord and fortepiano*, viii/1 (Autumn 1999), pp.3-10

-------, 'Jan Ladislav Dussek and his music for the extended keyboard compass', *Harpsichord and fortepiano*, ix/2 (Summer 2001), pp.8-15

Penelope Cave, 'Dance to the Music of Time [Delius, *Dance for Harpsichord*]', *Harpsichord and fortepiano*, vi/1 (May 1997), pp.7-9

-------, 'Practice Matters: Preparing the performing score to ease communication between the notes, the brain and the fingers', *Harpsichord and fortepiano*, ix/2 (Summer 2001), pp.16-19

-------, 'Keyboard Instruments & Quotation: Using a Quotation from C.P.E. Bach', *Harpsichord and fortepiano*, x/2 (Spring 2006), pp.19-20

-------, Bridget Cunningham, Elaine Comparone, Pamela Nash, 'New Music Focus', *Harpsichord and fortepiano*, xii/1 (Autumn 2007), pp.22-29

-------, 'Scarlatti Sonatas, Step by Step', *Harpsichord and fortepiano*, xii/2 (Spring 2008), pp.27-29

-------, 'Jane Austen and the Square Piano', *Harpsichord and fortepiano*, xvi/2 (Spring 2012), pp.4-6

Jane Chapman, 'The Challenge of New Music', *Harpsichord and fortepiano*, v/1 (October 1994), pp.7-13

-------, 'The Oriental Miscellany and the Hindustani Air: "Wild but Pleasing when Understood"', *Harpsichord and fortepiano*, xvii/2 (Spring 2013), pp.24-30

Terrence Charlston, 'An Introduction to Restoration Keyboard Music', *Harpsichord and fortepiano*, x/2 (Spring 2006), pp.26-36

-------, 'An Introduction to Restoration Keyboard Music II: Bryne, Roberts and Moss', *Harpsichord and fortepiano*, xi/1 (Autumn 2006), pp.14-27

-------, 'The *Orgelbüchlein* as pedal clavichord music', *Harpsichord & fortepiano*, xxvii/1 (Autumn 2022), pp.11-15

-------, 'A perspective on historical keyboard playing in the UK', *Harpsichord & fortepiano*, xxviii/1 (Autumn 2023), pp.26-27

Jane Clark, 'The Architecture of the Ordres [Couperin]', *Harpsichord and fortepiano*, x/2 (Spring 2006), pp.21-25

Kathryn Cok, 'A Quest for Music: Treasures from the University of Leiden Library Revealed, with a Special Focus on Dutch Music 1650-1750', *Harpsichord and fortepiano*, x/2 (Spring 2006), pp.37

-------, '"Eloquent Fingers": indications and implications of fingering in Sweelinck's keyboard music', *Harpsichord & fortepiano*, xxvi/2 (Spring 2022), pp.4-9

Grant Colburn with Micaela Schmitz, 'Everything New is Old Again – Part I', *Harpsichord and fortepiano*, xiv/1 (Autumn 2009), pp.18-23

-------, Fernando De Luca, Micaela Schmitz, 'Everything New is Old Again – Part II', *Harpsichord and fortepiano*, xiv/2 (Spring 2010), pp.20-29

Neil Coleman, 'Mozart and the Clavier', *Harpsichord and fortepiano*, xi/2 (Spring 2007), pp.20-30

-------, 'Mozart and the Clavier – a Supplement', *Harpsichord and fortepiano*, xii/1 (Autumn 2007), pp.30-34

C. F. Colt, 'An Interesting Early Forte-Piano', *The English Harpsichord Magazine*, i/7 (October 1976), pp.198-201

John Collins, 'Buxtehude's Works for Stringed Keyboard Instruments', *Harpsichord and fortepiano*, xi/2 (Spring 2007), pp.31-40

-------, 'An Overview of the Keyboard Music of Bernardo Pasquini (1637-1710)', *Harpsichord and fortepiano*, xv/1 (Autumn 2010), pp.17-24

-------, 'Composer anniversaries in 2020', *Harpsichord & fortepiano*, xxiv/2 (Spring 2020), pp.24-27

-------, 'Composer Anniversaries 2021', *Harpsichord & fortepiano*, xxv/2 (Spring 2021), pp.28-31

-------, 'Composer anniversaries in 2022', *Harpsichord & fortepiano*, xxvi/2 (Spring 2022), pp.31-34

-------, 'Composer Anniversaries in 2023', *Harpsichord & fortepiano*, xxvii/2 (Spring 2023), pp.31-33

Warwick Henry Cole, 'Collections – Finchcocks', *The Harpsichord and Fortepiano Magazine*, iv/3 (April 1987), pp.63-65

-------, 'Americus Backers: Original Forte Piano Maker', *The Harpsichord and Fortepiano Magazine*, iv/4 (October 1987), pp.79-85

Elaine Comparone, Penelope Cave, Bridget Cunningham, Pamela Nash, 'New Music Focus', *Harpsichord and fortepiano*, xii/1 (Autumn 2007), pp.22-29

Bridget Cunningham, Penelope Cave, Elaine Comparone, Pamela Nash, 'New Music Focus', *Harpsichord and fortepiano*, xii/1 (Autumn 2007), pp.22-29

Rebecca Cypess, 'Fortepiano-harpsichord duos in two eighteenth-century salons', *Harpsichord and fortepiano*, xxii/2 (Spring 2018), pp.20-25

D

Stephen Daw, 'Back to Bach: *Das Wohltemperirte Clavier* revisited', *Harpsichord and fortepiano*, v/2 (April 1995), pp.11-15

P. Deen, 'Quick Jacks for Amateurs', *The English Harpsichord Magazine*, i/3 (October 1974), pp.84-86

Fernando De Luca, Grant Colburn, Micaela Schmitz, 'Everything New is Old Again – Part II', *Harpsichord and fortepiano*, xiv/2 (Spring 2010), pp.20-29

Pieter Dirksen, 'Couperin's *Misterieuse* Fourth Harpsichord Book', *Harpsichord & fortepiano*, xxiv/1 (Autumn 2019), pp.18-23

Claudio Di Veroli, 'Did Couperin ever play a trill before the beat?', *Harpsichord and fortepiano*, vi/1 (May 1997), pp.20-22

-------, 'Early keyboards in Argentina', *Harpsichord and fortepiano*, vi/2 (November 1997), pp.20-21

-------, 'Inégalité and Rameau's Concerts: a case of "Ille dixit"?', *Harpsichord and fortepiano*, viii/2 (Spring 2000), pp.28-34

-------, 'Tuning the témpérament ordinare', *Harpsichord and fortepiano*, x/1 (Autumn 2002), pp.22-29

-------, 'Valotti as the Ideal German Good Temperament', *Harpsichord and fortepiano*, xv/1 (Autumn 2010), pp.9-14

-------, 'Optimising Harpsichord Staggering', *Harpsichord and fortepiano*, xvi/2 (Spring 2012), pp.8-13

-------, 'A measured approach to J.S. Bach's Stylus Phantasticus', *Harpsichord and fortepiano*, xxi/2 (Spring 2017), pp.17-26

-------, 'Accurate meantone tuning based on Fogliano', *Harpsichord and fortepiano*, xxiii/1 (Autumn 2018), pp.16-20

-------, 'Baroque Keyboard Fingering and Present-Day Practice', *Harpsichord and fortepiano*, xxiii/2 (Spring 2019), pp.27-34

-------, 'Performing François Couperin's *Les Baricades Mistérieuses*', *Harpsichord & fortepiano*, xxiv/2 (Spring 2020), pp.15-19

-------, '1741: three masterworks of diversity', *Harpsichord & fortepiano*, xxvi/2 (Spring 2022), pp.21-26

-------, 'Forkel's Bach revisited', *Harpsichord & fortepiano*, xxvii/2 (Spring 2023), pp.12-19

D. E. Dodge, 'Bach and the German Clavier', *The English Harpsichord Magazine*, ii/3 (October 1978), pp.67-71

-------, 'The Identity of Bach's Clavier', *The English Harpsichord Magazine*, ii/5 (October 1979), pp.116-119

William Dow, 'Two Harpsichords by Elpidio Gregori', *The Harpsichord and Fortepiano Magazine*, iv/6 (October 1988), pp.140-145

E

Dominic Eckersley, 'Vermeer's Ruckers Muselar Virginal: Vermeer's Painting of a Ruckers Muselar Virginal in *The Music Lesson* c. 1662-65', *Harpsichord and fortepiano*, xvix/2 (Spring 2015), pp.31-43

-------, 'Vermeer's Ruckers Muselar Virginal: Vermeer's Painting Of A Ruckers Muselar Virginal In The Music Lesson c. 1662-65. New Evidence: The Smoking Gun', *Harpsichord and fortepiano*, xx/1 (Autumn 2015), pp.8-10

L. A. Esteves Pereria, 'The Instrumental Museum – Lisbon', *The English Harpsichord Magazine*, i/7 (October 1976), pp.197-198

-------, 'An Octave Harpsichord at the Instrumental Museum - Lisbon', *The English Harpsichord Magazine*, ii/2 (April 1978), pp.30-32

-------, 'A Forte-piano at the Instrumental Museum – Lisbon', *The English Harpsichord Magazine*, iii/4 (April 1983), pp.67-70

-------, 'Two small Organs revived', *The English Harpsichord Magazine*, iii/4 (April 1983), pp.73-76

-------, 'Another Burkat Tchudi Harpichord Found', *The English Harpsichord Magazine*, iii/6 (April 1984), p.119

David Evans, 'Copying a 17th-Century French Harpsichord', *Harpsichord and fortepiano*, xix/1 (Autumn 2014), p.6

F

Elaine Fuller, Richard Troeger, 'Landowska and the Pleyel pianos: a Foot(pedalled) note to the Harpsichord Revival', *Harpsichord and fortepiano*, xviii/2 (Spring 2014), pp.22-33

G

Mark Ganullin, 'An Overview of Pedal Harpsichord Recordings', *Harpsichord and fortepiano*, xi/2 (Spring 2007), pp.41-44

Jonathan Garland, 'The John Loosemore Centre for Organ and Early Music', *The English Harpsichord Magazine*, ii/6 (April 1980), pp.134-136

Gerald Gifford, 'Viscount Fitzwilliam and the English "Scarlatti Sect"', *The Harpsichord and Fortepiano Magazine*, iv/5 (April 1988), pp.113-116

-------, 'Some rare sources of Georgian harpsichord music in the Library of Arnold Dolmetsch (1858-1940)', *Harpsichord and fortepiano*, ix/2 (Summer 2001), pp.20-25

-------, 'Eighteenth Century English Publications of Keyboard Music in the Library of Burghley House, Stamford', *Harpsichord and fortepiano*, x/1 (Autumn 2002), pp.16-21

Martha Goodway, 'Fortepiano kapsels old and new', *Harpsichord and fortepiano*, vi/1 (May 1997), pp.13-16

Göran Grahn, 'A Bone of Contention: Should we stop restoring and playing original instruments?', *Harpsichord and fortepiano*, v/1 (October 1994), pp.27-28

Daniel Grimwood, 'Keyboard Temperament in the Nineteenth Century: The Well Tempered Romantic', *Harpsichord and fortepiano*, xiii/2 (Spring 2009), pp.28-32

H

David Hackett, 'Ivory Sales in the United Kingdom and European Community', *Harpsichord & fortepiano*, xxvii/1 (Autumn 2022), pp.23-24

Jenny Haylett, '"Take Six Eggs…": Making and using egg tempera on harpsichord soundboards', *Harpsichord and fortepiano*, v/2 (April 1995), pp.20-22

Pamela Hickman, 'Elisabeth-Claude Jacquet De La Guerre', *Harpsichord and fortepiano*, xvi/1 (Autumn 2011), pp.12-14

Asako Hirabayashi, 'The Authority of the Bevin table in the interpretation of ornament signs in Elizabethan virginal music', *Harpsichord and fortepiano*, ix/1 (Spring 2001), pp.24-30

Alison Holloway, 'Underground Movement [Harley Foundation]', *Harpsichord and fortepiano*, vii/1 (June 1998), pp.35-38

-------, '*pian'e fortino*: The Neumeyer Collection and its curator', *Harpsichord and fortepiano*, vii/1 (Winter 1998), pp.35-38

\-\-\-\-\-\-\-, 'Renaissance Harpsichord Renaissance: Philip Pickett's approach to performance practice and why he commissioned the Trasuntino copy', *Harpsichord and fortepiano*, ix/1 (Spring 2001), pp.3-6

Peter Holman, 'The harpsichord in 19th-century England', *Harpsichord & fortepiano*, xxiv/2 (Spring 2020), pp.4-14

Edgar Hunt, 'Tuning and Temperament', *The English Harpsichord Magazine*, i/7 (October 1976), pp.201-204

\-\-\-\-\-\-\-, 'A Harpsichord Odyssey (1)', *The English Harpsichord Magazine*, ii/8 (April 1981), pp.190-194

\-\-\-\-\-\-\-, 'A Harpsichord Odyssey (II)', *The English Harpsichord Magazine*, iii/1 (October 1981), pp.4-7

\-\-\-\-\-\-\-, 'Telemann's Harpsichord Music', *The English Harpsichord Magazine*, iii/1 (October 1981), p.16

\-\-\-\-\-\-\-, 'The Virginal at the Museum of London', *The English Harpsichord Magazine*, iii/4 (April 1983), p.79

\-\-\-\-\-\-\-, 'On choosing a Harpsichord', *The English Harpsichord Magazine*, iii/5 (October 1983), pp.97-98

\-\-\-\-\-\-\-, 'Musings on the Muselar', *The (English) Harpsichord Magazine*, iii/7 (October 1984), pp.143-144

Desmond Hunter, 'The Position of Grace Signs in MS. Sources of English Virginal Music', *The English Harpsichord Magazine*, iii/5 (October 1983), pp.82-91

\-\-\-\-\-\-\-, 'Further Light on Early Keyboard Fingerings', *The (English) Harpsichord Magazine*, iv/1 (October 1985), pp.2-7

\-\-\-\-\-\-\-, 'The Keyboard Music of Hugh Facy', *The Harpsichord and Fortepiano Magazine*, iv/7 (April 1989), pp.173-177

I

Paul Y. Irvin, 'An Approach to Recreating Historical Sound: Part 1', *Harpsichord and fortepiano*, xii/2 (Spring 2008), pp.33-38

\-\-\-\-\-\-\-, 'An Approach to Recreating Historical Sound: Part II', *Harpsichord and fortepiano*, xiii/1 (Autumn 2008), pp.21-27

\-\-\-\-\-\-\-, 'Modifying Modern Harpsichord Dampers', *Harpsichord and fortepiano*, xiv/2 (Spring 2010), p.30-34

\-\-\-\-\-\-\-, 'Tailoring the Sound of your Keyboard Instrument, Part 1', *Harpsichord and fortepiano*, xvi/1 (Autumn 2011), pp.27-32

\-\-\-\-\-\-\-, 'Tailoring the Sound of your Keyboard Instrument, Part II', *Harpsichord and fortepiano*, xvi/2 (Spring 2012), pp.20-26

\-\-\-\-\-\-\-, 'Using Appropriate Pitches and Stringing Schedules', *Harpsichord and fortepiano*, xvii/2 (Spring 2013), pp.13-23

\-\-\-\-\-\-\-, 'Tailoring the Sound of your Keyboard Instrument Part IV: Musical Pins', *Harpsichord and fortepiano*, xviii/1 (Autumn 2013), pp.17-23

K

-------, 'Modern vs historical harpsichord plucking', *Harpsichord & fortepiano*, xxviii/1 (Autumn 2023), pp.19-21

Herbert Anton Kellner, 'Was Bach a Mathematician?', *The English Harpsichord Magazine*, ii/2 (April 1978), pp.32-36

-------, 'Das Wohltemperierte Clavier: Tuning & Musical Structure', *The English Harpsichord Magazine*, ii/6 (April 1980), pp.137-140

-------, 'The Mathematical Architecture of Bach's Goldberg Variations', *The English Harpsichord Magazine*, ii/8 (April 1981), pp.183-189

-------, 'Is there an Enigma in Werckmeister's "Musicalische Temperatur"?', *The (English) Harpsichord Magazine*, iii/7 (October 1984), pp.134-136

-------, 'One typographical Enigma in Werckmeister, "Musicalische Temperatur"', *The (English) Harpsichord Magazine*, iii/8 (April 1985), pp.146-151

-------, 'Did Werckmeister already know the tuning of J. S. Bach for the "48"?', *The (English) Harpsichord Magazine*, iv/1 (October 1985), pp.7-11

-------, 'How Bach quantified his well-tempered tuning within the FOUR DUETS', *The English Harpsichord Magazine*, iv/2 (1986), pp.21-27

John Khouri, 'Rediscovering Clementi's *Gradus ad Parnassum*: A New perspective from the Early English Piano', *Harpsichord and fortepiano*, xvii/1 (Autumn 2012), pp.11-14

Andreas Kilström, 'The Hudiksvall Mietke', Andreas Kilström, *Harpsichord and fortepiano*, v/1 (October 1994), pp.15-18

Richard Kingston, Caperton Andersson, 'Makers' Reports: The Birth of a Harpsichord: Richard Kingston's Opus #333', *Harpsichord and fortepiano*, xiv/2 (Spring 2010), pp.4-5

Christopher Kite, 'Playing Mozart On The Fortepiano', *The Harpsichord and Fortepiano Magazine*, iv/3 (April 1987), pp.52-55

Francis Knights, Pablo Padilla and Dan Tidhar, 'Chambonnières versus Louis Couperin: attributing the F major Chaconne', *Harpsichord and fortepiano*, xxii/1 (Autumn 2017), pp.28-32

Francis Knights, 'Learning 'The 48', *Harpsichord and fortepiano*, xxiii/1 (Autumn 2018), pp.21-31

-------, 'The musician's bookshelf: J. S. Bach', *Harpsichord & fortepiano*, xxiv/2 (Spring 2020), p.32

-------, 'The keyboard music of Charles Burney', *Harpsichord & fortepiano*, xxv/2 (Spring 2021), pp.13-23

-------, '50 years of *Harpsichord & Fortepiano*', *Harpsichord & fortepiano*, xxviii/1 (Autumn 2023), pp.4-7

Katalin Komlos, 'On the New Fortepiano in Contemporary German Musical Writings', *The Harpsichord and Fortepiano Magazine*, iv/6 (October 1988), pp.134-139

Ton Koopman, '"My Lady Nevell's Book" and Old Fingerings', *The English Harpsichord Magazine*, ii/1 (October 1977), pp.5-10

John Koster, 'In the Beginning was the Harpsichord', *Harpsichord & fortepiano*, xxviii/1 (Autumn 2023), pp.22-25

Rudolph Kremer, 'Organ Restoration in Florence, *The English Harpsichord Magazine*, ii/2 (April 1978), pp.37-39

Mark Kroll, 'Swimming upstream: Reflections of an American harpsichordist from across "The Pond"', *Harpsichord & fortepiano*, xxviii/1 (Autumn 2023), pp.35-38

L

Elisabetta Lanzoni, 'A Path towards Lid Decoration', *Harpsichord and fortepiano*, xiii/1 (Autumn 2008), p.9

Dave Law, 'Harpsichord Building: I. Preparing the Action for Voicing', *The Harpsichord Magazine*, i/1 (October 1973), pp.23-25

------, 'Harpsichord Building: II. Voicing and Regulating', *The English Harpsichord Magazine*, i/2 (April 1974), pp.53-57

------, 'Harpsichord Building: Preparing the Action for Voicing', *The English Harpsichord Magazine*, iii/5 (October 1983), pp.98-102, 96

------, 'Maintenance: String Replacement', *Harpsichord and fortepiano*, x/2 (Spring 2006), pp.14-18

------, 'Harpsichord Regulation', *Harpsichord and fortepiano*, xiii/1 (Autumn 2008), pp.17-20

------, 'Harpsichord Regulation, Part II', *Harpsichord and fortepiano*, xiii/2 (Spring 2009), pp.24-27

Richard Leigh Harris, 'Some thoughts on Playing the Goldberg Variations, BWV 988', *Harpsichord and fortepiano*, xiv/2 (Spring 2010), pp.16-19

John Lester, 'The Musical Mechanisms of Arnaut de Zwolle', *The English Harpsichord Magazine*, iii/3 (October 1982), pp.35-41

Richard Lester, 'The Performer's Approach to Scarlatti', *The English Harpsichord Magazine*, i/8 (April 1977), pp.223-226

------, 'Thoughts on Scarlatti's Essercizi per Gravicembalo', *The English Harpsichord Magazine*, ii/1 (October 1977), pp.10-12, 17-18

------, 'Flamenco Sketches: Part 1 [Scarlatti]', *Harpsichord and fortepiano*, xi/1 (Autumn 2006), pp.28-33

------, 'Flamenco Sketches: Part 2 [Scarlatti]', *Harpsichord and fortepiano*, xi/2 (Spring 2007), pp.12-16

------, 'Frescobaldi Unmasked: Unravelling Complexities of Interpretation within the Toccatas', *Harpsichord and fortepiano*, xiii/2 (Spring 2009), pp.10-19

------, 'Fingers Crossed: Girolamo Diruta's *Il Transilvano* (1593): A Re-evaluation', *Harpsichord and fortepiano*, xvix/2 (Spring 2015), pp.15-26

------, 'Trills and frills, a variety of inventions: the North Italian art of Diminutione and Tremoli', *Harpsichord and fortepiano*, xx/1 (Autumn 2015), pp.11-26

------, 'Registration matters: analyzing Italian Renaissance registration', *Harpsichord and fortepiano*, xxi/1 (Autumn 2016), pp.15-21

-------, 'Flamenco sketches (revisited) [Scarlatti]', *Harpsichord & fortepiano*, xxvi/1 (Autumn 2021), pp.9-15

-------, 'Music and criticism: Revisiting George Malcolm's thoughts on authenticity', *Harpsichord & fortepiano*, xxviii/1 (Autumn 2023), pp.28-30

M. R. Levoi and R. P. Williams, 'The Wearing Properties of Harpsichord Plectra', *The English Harpsichord Magazine*, i/6 (April 1976), pp.172-174

Christopher D. Lewis, 'The challenges of a modern recording on a Pleyel harpsichord', *Harpsichord & fortepiano*, xxv/1 (Autumn 2020), pp.15-20

Laurence Libin, 'The Metropolitan Museum of Art', *The Harpsichord and Fortepiano Magazine*, iv/7 (April 1989), pp.178-184

-------, 'Clavichords at Vassar College', *Harpsichord & fortepiano*, xxvii/2 (Spring 2023), pp.20-25

Mark Lindley, 'Tuning Systems for 12-note Keyboard Instruments', *The English Harpsichord Magazine*, ii/1 (October 1977), pp.13-15

-------, 'Ammerbach's 1583 Exercises', *The English Harpsichord Magazine*, iii/4 (April 1983), pp.58-66

-------, 'Early Keyboard Fingerings: A select Bibliography', *The (English) Harpsichord Magazine*, iii/8 (April 1985), pp.155-161 (see also EHM iv/1 (October 1985), p.15)

Catherine Lorigan, '"Queen Elizabeth's Virginals": from Venice to the Victoria & Albert Museum', *Harpsichord & fortepiano*, xxv/2 (Spring 2021), pp.4-13

Richard Luckett, 'The English Virginals: I', *The English Harpsichord Magazine*, i/3 (October 1974), pp.69-72

M

[George Malcolm], Richard Lester, 'Music and criticism: Revisiting George Malcolm's thoughts on authenticity', *Harpsichord & fortepiano*, xxviii/1 (Autumn 2023), pp.28-30

Kevin Malone, 'The Naked Truth: Composing for the Harpsichord', *Harpsichord and fortepiano*, vii/1 (Winter 1998), pp.5-9

Richard Maunder, 'Keyboard Instruments in Haydn's Vienna', *Harpsichord and fortepiano*, vii/1 (June 1998), pp.5-10

Thomas McGeary, 'Early English Harpsichord Building: A Reassessment', *The Harpsichord Magazine*, i/1 (October 1973), pp.7-19, 30

-------, 'Early Eighteenth-Century English Harpsichord Tuning and Stringing', *The English Harpsichord Magazine*, iii/2 (April 1982), pp.18-22

-------, 'Michael Thomas (1922–2022): a centenary tribute', *Harpsichord & fortepiano*, xxvii/2 (Spring 2023), pp.4-11

Paul McNulty, 'Introduction to the Making of a Pleyel', *Harpsichord and fortepiano*, xiv/2 (Spring 2010), pp.6-7

-------, 'Introduction to the Making of a Pleyel (Part II)', *Harpsichord and fortepiano*, xv/1 (Autumn 2010), p.6

-------, 'Making a Boisselot', *Harpsichord and fortepiano*, xvi/1 (Autumn 2011), pp.5-6

Nicholas Mitchell, 'The 1531 Trasuntino Harpsichord in a Universal European Pitch System', *Harpsichord and fortepiano*, ix/1 (Spring 2001), pp.7-13

Kenneth Mobbs, 'English Upright Grands and Cabinet Pianos', *Harpsichord and fortepiano*, xi/1 (Autumn 2006), pp.44-50

Mary Mobbs, 'Soundboard painting: The Traditional Touch', *Harpsichord and fortepiano*, v/3 (October 1995), pp.31-32

-------, 'Painting Harpsichord Soundboards – my memories', *Harpsichord and fortepiano*, xiii/1 (Autumn 2008), pp.10-16

Peter Mole, 'The Bentside Spinets of Stephen Keene and his School', *Harpsichord and fortepiano*, xiv/1 (Autumn 2009), pp.8-17

Brian Morgan, 'Master Brian his Virginall [Lodewijk Theeuwes]', *The English Harpsichord Magazine*, ii/5 (October 1979), pp.114-115

Charles Mould, 'The Broadwood Books: I', *The Harpsichord Magazine*, i/1 (October 1973), pp.19-23

-------, 'An Early-Eighteenth-century Harpsichord by Thomas Barton', *The English Harpsichord Magazine*, i/2 (April 1974), pp.36-38

-------, 'The Broadwood Books; II', *The English Harpsichord Magazine*, i/2 (April 1974), pp.47-53

-------, 'Towards Boalch III', *The Harpsichord and Fortepiano Magazine*, iv/3 (April 1987), pp.56-59

Daniel Moult, 'Ten Top Historic Organs', *Harpsichord and fortepiano*, xvii/2 (Spring 2013), pp.31-34

N

Pamela Nash, 'Bach Transcribed: A Study in Two Parts', *Harpsichord and fortepiano*, vii/1 (Winter 1998), pp.39-43

-------, 'Bach Transcribed: Part Two', *Harpsichord and fortepiano*, viii/1 (Autumn 1999), pp.23-26

-------, 'Bach Transcribed: Part Three', *Harpsichord and fortepiano*, viii/2 (Spring 2000), pp.19-23

-------, Penelope Cave, Bridget Cunningham, Elaine Comparone, 'New Music Focus', *Harpsichord and fortepiano*, xii/1 (Autumn 2007), pp.22-29

-------, 'A commemoration of Elizabeth de la Porte', *Harpsichord & fortepiano*, xxv/2 (Spring 2021), pp.35-36

Simon Neal, 'Monteverdi on the road', *Harpsichord and fortepiano*, v/1 (October 1994), pp.22-25

Mafalda Nejmeddine, 'Portuguese keyboard music from the second half of the 18th century', *Harpsichord & fortepiano*, xxvi/1 (Autumn 2021), pp.4-8

Kah-Ming Ng, 'Rudolf Straube', *Harpsichord and fortepiano*, xv/2 (Spring 2011), pp.27-28

Chris Nobbs, 'A Seventeenth Century French Harpsichord', *The Harpsichord and Fortepiano Magazine*, iv/3 (April 1987), pp.46-51 [see also *HF* iv/4 (October 1987), pp.102-103]

-------, 'A Seventeenth Century French Harpsichord?', *The Harpsichord and Fortepiano Magazine*, iv/4 (October 1987), pp.102-103

Barbara Norton, 'The Once and Future Harpsichord: The Aliénor Competition for Composition', *Harpsichord and fortepiano*, xiii/1 (Autumn 2008), pp.6-7

Giulia Nuti, '"…dovendosi sonare piu piano, che sij possibile…": style in Italian harpsichord basso continuo realization', *Harpsichord and fortepiano*, vii/1 (Winter 1998), pp.18-26

P

Pablo Padilla, Francis Knights, Dan Tidhar, 'Chambonnières versus Louis Couperin: attributing the F major Chaconne', *Harpsichord and fortepiano*, xxii/1 (Autumn 2017), pp.28-32

John Paul, 'Harpsichord Tone Colour', *The English Harpsichord Magazine*, ii/1 (October 1977), pp.22-26

-------, 'A Modern Upright Harpsichord', *The English Harpsichord Magazine*, ii/5 (October 1979), pp.124-125

Julian Perkins, '"An Eagle over Falcons": recording harpsichord music by John Worgan (1724-1790)', *Harpsichord & fortepiano*, xxvi/1 (Autumn 2021), pp.29-30

John Phillips, 'A Practical Guide to Quilling', *Harpsichord and fortepiano*, xviii/1 (Autumn 2013), pp.24-31

Philip Pickett, 'The Brandenburg Concertos: A New Interpretation', *Harpsichord and fortepiano*, vi/2 (November 1997), pp.22-32

-------, 'Behind the Mask: Continuo in Monteverdi's *L'Orfeo*', *Harpsichord and fortepiano*, vii/1 (Winter 1998), pp.10-16

R

John Raymond, 'St. Cecilia's Hall And The Russell Collection', *The Harpsichord and Fortepiano Magazine*, iv/4 (October 1987), pp.86-91

Marc Reichow and Richard Sims, '*Philibuster*: New music for the fortepiano', *Harpsichord and fortepiano*, v/3 (October 1995), pp.23-29

J. J. K. Rhodes and W. R. Thomas, 'Harpsichords…with all the different-siz'd wire used in that instrument (I)', *The English Harpsichord Magazine*, iii/6 (April 1984), pp.116-118

-------, W. R. Thomas, 'Harpsichords...with all the different-siz'd wire used in that instrument (II)', *The (English) Harpsichord Magazine*, iii/7 (October 1984), pp.130-133

-------, W. R. Thomas, 'Harpsichords...with all the different-siz'd wire used in that instrument (III)', *The (English) Harpsichord Magazine*, iii/8 (April 1985), pp.152-154

J. A. Richard, 'The Pleyel Harpsichord', *The English Harpsichord Magazine*, ii/5 (October 1979), pp.110-113

Martin Robertson, 'The vital rôle of humidity', *Harpsichord and fortepiano*, vi/1 (May 1997), p.27

David Roblou, 'Aspects of Thorough Bass', *The Harpsichord and Fortepiano Magazine*, iv/5 (April 1988), pp.106-112

María Virginia Rolfo, 'A Glimpse of the Tagliavini Collection of Musical Instruments', *Harpsichord and fortepiano*, xvi/1 (Autumn 2011), pp.15-20

S

Huw Saunders, 'A triple-strung 17th-century Italian harpsichord', *Harpsichord and fortepiano*, xxii/1 (Autumn 2017), pp.20-27

Leonard Schick, 'Harpsichords in Bach's Germany: an overview', *Harpsichord & fortepiano*, xxvi/2 (Spring 2022), pp.10-20

Micaela Schmitz, 'Why is the "Great *In Nomine*" great? [John Bull]', *Harpsichord and fortepiano*, x/2 (Spring 2006), pp.45-51

-------, Grant Colburn, 'Everything New is Old Again – Part I', *Harpsichord and fortepiano*, xiv/1 (Autumn 2009), pp.18-23

-------, Grant Colburn, Fernando De Luca, 'Everything New is Old Again – Part II', *Harpsichord and fortepiano*, xiv/2 (Spring 2010), pp.20-29

-------, 'Revisiting keyboard technique', *Harpsichord and fortepiano*, xxi/2 (Spring 2017), pp.28-31

David Schulenberg, '"Because they could never have equaled their father in his style": creativity at the keyboard in the Bach family', *Harpsichord & fortepiano*, xxiv/1 (Autumn 2019), pp.4-7

Kerstin Schwarz, 'The *Clavecin Roïal* and the first copy in modern times', *Harpsichord & fortepiano*, xxv/1 (Autumn 2020), pp.11-14

Maxim Serebrennikov, '"Ziegler Variations": On the Goldberg Polonaises: In Search of the Author', *Harpsichord and fortepiano*, xiv/2 (Spring 2010), pp.9-15

-------, 'Book for Thoroughbass (1786) owned by Ms. Avdot'ja Ivanova: Pages from one lady's music album during the period of Catherine the Great', *Harpsichord and fortepiano*, xvi/1 (Autumn 2011), pp.21-26

Paul Simmonds, 'The Pantalon Clavichord: Resonance from the Eighteenth Century', *Harpsichord and fortepiano*, xi/1 (Autumn 2006), pp.38-43

-------, 'Keyboard instruments – some collective thoughts', *Harpsichord & fortepiano*, xxvi/1 (Autumn 2021), pp.21-28

-------, 'Identifying clavichord repertoire', *Harpsichord & fortepiano*, xxvii/1 (Autumn 2022), pp.16-22

-------, 'An unusual square piano "ravalement"', *Harpsichord & fortepiano*, xxvii/2 (Spring 2023), pp.26-30

Richard Sims, Marc Reichow, '*Philibuster*: New music for the fortepiano', *Harpsichord and fortepiano*, v/3 (October 1995), pp.23-29

Carl Sloane, 'The Cent System: with an easy method of calculation', *Harpsichord and fortepiano*, v/3 (October 1995), pp.15-16

-------, 'Mean as they come: Clues in the elucidation of Handel's harpsichord temperament', *Harpsichord and fortepiano*, v/3 (October 1995), pp.17-19

-------, 'Handel's Temperament – A Revised View', *Harpsichord and fortepiano*, vi/2 (November 1997), p.35

David J. Smith, 'Full Circle? Observations on keyboard music to c.1630 in Musica Britannica and some thoughts about the future', *Harpsichord & fortepiano*, xxviii/1 (Autumn 2023), pp.42-44

Eleanor Smith, 'The Current State of Claviorgan Research', *Harpsichord & fortepiano*, xxiv/1 (Autumn 2019), pp.8-11

Calimerio Soares, 'The harpsichord in Brazil', *Harpsichord and fortepiano*, xi/2 (Spring 2007), pp.17-19

-------, 'Composing *Toccata de Roça* for Solo Harpsichord', *Harpsichord and fortepiano*, xii/2 (Spring 2008), pp.15-26

Andrew Stewart, 'Losing their heads?', *Harpsichord and fortepiano*, ix/1 (Spring 2001), pp.14-15

P. Sween, 'The Nineteenth-Century View of the Old Harpsichord', *The English Harpsichord Magazine*, ii/4 (April 1979), pp.92-95

T

Maurizio Tarrini, 'Ligurian harpsichord investigated', *Harpsichord and fortepiano*, v/2 (April 1995), pp.33-34

Michael Thomas, 'The Fretted Clavichord', *The English Harpsichord Magazine*, i/2 (April 1974), pp.39-47

-------, 'Early French Harpsichords', *The English Harpsichord Magazine*, i/3 (October 1974), pp.73-84

-------, 'Venetian Harpsichords', *The English Harpsichord Magazine*, i/4 (April 1975), pp.109-120

-------, 'The Development of the Tuning and Tone Colour of an Instrument made in Venice about 1500', *The English Harpsichord Magazine*, i/5 (October 1975), pp.145-155

-------, 'The Tunings and Pitch of Early Clavichords', *The English Harpsichord Magazine*, i/6 (April 1976), pp.175-180

-------, 'The Harpsichord at the Courtauld Institute', *The English Harpsichord Magazine*, i/7 (October 1976), pp.194-197

-------, 'Notes and Corrections to former Articles and New Information', pp.211-219
Michael Thomas, 'Further Thoughts and Notes', *The English Harpsichord Magazine*, i/8 (April 1977), pp.223-235

-------, 'Thoughts on the Restoration of Harpsichords', *The English Harpsichord Magazine*, ii/3 (October 1978), pp.62-67

-------, 'The Upright Harpsichord', *The English Harpsichord Magazine*, ii/4 (April 1979), pp.84-92

-------, 'Harpsichords which have been found recently in France', *The English Harpsichord Magazine*, ii/7 (October 1980), pp.158-163

-------, 'Recent Harpsichord Restorations (I)', *The English Harpsichord Magazine*, iii/3 (October 1982), pp.45-48

-------, 'Recent Harpsichord Restorations (II)', *The English Harpsichord Magazine*, iii/4 (April 1983), pp.71-72, 79

-------, 'The temperament for Bach's "48"', *The English Harpsichord Magazine*, iv/2 (1986), pp.18-21

-------, 'The Fretted Clavichord', *The English Harpsichord Magazine*, iv/2 (1986), pp.33-44

W. R. Thomas, J. J. K. Rhodes, 'Harpsichords...with all the different-siz'd wire used in that instrument (I)', *The English Harpsichord Magazine*, iii/6 (April 1984), pp.116-118

-------, J. J. K. Rhodes, 'Harpsichords...with all the different-siz'd wire used in that instrument (II)', *The (English) Harpsichord Magazine*, iii/7 (October 1984), pp.130-133

-------, J. J. K. Rhodes, 'Harpsichords...with all the different-siz'd wire used in that instrument (III)', *The (English) Harpsichord Magazine*, iii/8 (April 1985), pp.152-154

Peter Thresh, 'A Late Florentine Harpsichord Uncovered', *Harpsichord and fortepiano*, xiv/1 (Autumn 2009), pp.24-29

Dan Tidhar, Francis Knights, Pablo Padilla, 'Chambonnières versus Louis Couperin: attributing the F major Chaconne', *Harpsichord and fortepiano*, xxii/1 (Autumn 2017), pp.28-32

Marco Tiella, 'The Archicembalo of Nicola Vincentino', *The English Harpsichord Magazine*, i/5 (October 1975), pp.134-144

Kasia Tomczak-Feltrin, 'Le Clavecin en France', *Harpsichord and fortepiano*, xii/2 (Spring 2008), pp.30-32

Richard Troeger, 'Interpretation on Multiple Keyboards: From the Performer's Perspective', *Harpsichord and fortepiano*, xi/1 (Autumn 2006), pp.34-37

-------, 'Clavichords, Fretted & Unfretted', *Harpsichord and fortepiano*, xv/2 (Spring 2011), pp.19-26

-------, 'Texture and Playing Style in Classic Keyboard Music', *Harpsichord and fortepiano*, xvi/2 (Spring 2012), pp.27-32

-------, Elaine Fuller, 'Landowska and the Pleyel pianos: a Foot(pedalled) note to the Harpsichord Revival', *Harpsichord and fortepiano*, xviii/2 (Spring 2014), pp.22-33

-------, 'Landowska and the Clavichord', *Harpsichord and fortepiano*, xix/1 (Autumn 2014), pp.7-8

-------, 'The mid-nineteenth century Pleyel pianos: an appreciation', *Harpsichord and fortepiano*, xx/1 (Autumn 2015), pp.27-38

-------, 'The mid-nineteenth century Pleyel pianos: an appreciation, Part II', *Harpsichord and fortepiano*, xx/2 (Spring 2016), pp.22-32

-------, 'Unanswered questions: Bach, Forkel, *schellen*, and keyboard touch', *Harpsichord and fortepiano*, xxi/1 (Autumn 2016), pp.22-32

-------, 'Varied Dispositions', *Harpsichord & fortepiano*, xxiv/1 (Autumn 2019), pp.12-17

-------, 'Clavichord gatherings', *Harpsichord & fortepiano*, xxviii/1 (Autumn 2023), pp.31-34

Roy Truby, 'Elementary Harpsichord Technique', *The English Harpsichord Magazine*, i/5 (October 1975), pp.132-134

-------, 'Tuning and Temperaments', *The English Harpsichord Magazine*, i/8 (April 1977), p.235

W

Mimi Waitzman, 'Conservation conversation', *Harpsichord and fortepiano*, v/1 (October 1994), p.26

-------, 'Care of…: Regular maintenance of your keyboard', *Harpsichord and fortepiano*, v/1 (October 1994), pp.41-42

-------, 'Care of…: Regular maintenance of your keyboard', *Harpsichord and fortepiano*, v/2 (April 1995), pp.40-41

-------, 'Care of…: Regular maintenance of your keyboard', *Harpsichord and fortepiano*, v/3 (October 1995), pp.38-39

Peter Watchorn, 'Isolde Ahlgrimm and Vienna's Historic Keyboard Revival', *Harpsichord and fortepiano*, vi/2 (November 1997), pp.10-17

-------, 'Isolde Ahlgrimm: discography, performers, publications and instruments', *Harpsichord and fortepiano*, vii/1 (June 1998), pp.14-22

John Watson, 'The venerable "Boalch" - ready for its next 70 years', *Harpsichord & fortepiano*, xxviii/1 (Autumn 2023), pp.39-41

Robert Webb, 'Techniques of Baroque Accompaniment', *Harpsichord and fortepiano*, vii/1 (Winter 1998), pp.28-34

Stephen Wessel, 'The Claviorganum in England', *The English Harpsichord Magazine*, i/8 (April 1977), pp.226-233

R. P. Williams, M. R. Levoi, 'The Wearing Properties of Harpsichord Plectra', *The English Harpsichord Magazine*, i/6 (April 1976), pp.172-174

Glen Wilson, 'Claudio Merulo: Two biographical notes', *Harpsichord & fortepiano*, xxvii/1 (Autumn 2022), pp.4-10

Allan Winkler, 'Early keyboard technology instruction in the US', *Harpsichord & fortepiano*, xxvi/1 (Autumn 2021), pp.21-32

David Winston, '…Or should good restoration still be carried out?', *Harpsichord and fortepiano*, v/1 (October 1994), p.29

Paula Woods, 'Windebank's Virginall: A Lost Ruckers Harpsichord', *Harpsichord and fortepiano*, ix/1 (Spring 2001), pp.16-23

Andrew Woolley, 'William Babell's recently discovered toccatas', *Harpsichord & fortepiano*, xxvi/2 (Spring 2022), pp.27-30

Dennis Woolley, 'The Haward Harpsichord at Knole', *The English Harpsichord Magazine*, iii/1 (October 1981), pp.2-3

www.ingramcontent.com/pod-product-compliance
Lightning Source LLC
Chambersburg PA
CBHW081559040426
42444CB00012B/3169